Ruby Programming for Beginners

An Introduction to Learning Ruby Programming with Tutorials and Hands-On Examples

Legal & Disclaimer

The information contained in this book and its contents is not designed to replace or take the place of any form of medical or professional advice; and is not meant to replace the need for independent medical, financial, legal or other professional advice or services, as may be required. The content and information in this book has been provided for educational and entertainment purposes only.

The content and information contained in this book has been compiled from sources deemed reliable, and it is accurate to the best of the Author's knowledge, information, and belief. However, the Author cannot guarantee its accuracy and validity and cannot be held liable for any errors and/or omissions. Further, changes are periodically made to this book as and when needed. Where appropriate and/or necessary, you must consult a professional (including but not limited to your doctor, attorney, financial advisor or such other professional advisor) before using any of the suggested remedies, techniques, or information in this book.

Upon using the contents and information contained in this book, you agree to hold harmless the Author from and against any damages, costs, and expenses, including any legal fees potentially resulting from the application of any of the information provided by this book. This disclaimer applies to any loss, damages or injury caused by the use and application, whether directly or indirectly, of any advice or information presented, whether for breach of contract, tort, negligence, personal injury, criminal intent, or under any other cause of action.

You agree to accept all risks of using the information presented in this book.

You agree that by continuing to read this book, where appropriate and/or necessary, you shall consult a professional (including but not limited to your doctor, attorney, or financial advisor or such other advisor as needed) before using any of the suggested remedies, techniques, or information in this book.

Table of Contents

1. Introduction

Ruby is a cross-platform general purpose scripting language. Being a cross-platform language, it follows *write once, run everywhere* concept. When we say scripting language, in most cases, there is an interpreter which is responsible for executing the script. In this case, there is a Ruby interpreter which executes a Ruby script. Ruby supports multiple programming paradigms such as procedural, object-oriented and functional. This is a language that is easy to learn, read, understand and write. Hence it is often referred to as Programmer's best friend.

1.1 History

A ***Japanese*** computer scientist called ***Yukihiro Matsumoto*** started working on designing the Ruby language in 1993 and the first stable version of Ruby appeared in 1995. According to Matsumoto, Ruby is influenced by Perl, Smalltalk, Eiffel, Ada, Basic, and Lisp. The first version of Ruby was 0.95 released in 1995 followed by several stable versions such as Ruby 1.0 in 1996, Ruby 1.2 in 1998, Ruby 1.4 in 1999, Ruby 1.6 in 2000 and so on. At the time of writing this book (March 2020), the latest version is Ruby 2.7.

1.2 Supported Platforms

Yukihiro Matsumoto first started developing Ruby on ***4.3BSD***, later moved to ***SunOS v4*** and eventually to ***Linux***. Today, Ruby supports most well-known platforms such as ***Linux, Windows, MAC OS, BSD (FreeBSD, DragonFly BSD, etc.), Solaris, AIX, Windows Phone, Windows CE, Symbian, etc***. Ruby being a cross platform language, as long as there is no platform specific code in a program, a Ruby script written on one supported platform should work on another supported platform. For example, a script written on and for Linux should work on Windows without any problems.

Ruby interpreters are also available for ARM-Linux platforms. Which means running scripts on single board computers (SBC) such as ***Raspberry Pi, Beagleboard, Asus Tinkerboard S, Orange Pi, etc.*** is also possible. In the era of Cloud Computing, Ruby remains popular because of its power and ease of deployment on ***Virtual Machines (eg. AWS), Containers (eg. Docker), etc.***

1.3 Ruby Implementations

The implementation language of Ruby is C. However, no C programming knowledge is required to learn Ruby. The de-facto reference implementation of Ruby by Yukihiro Matsumoto himself is called ***Matz's Ruby Interpreter, MRI or CRuby*** and is open-source. Alongside this, there are many more alternate implementations such as ***JRuby*** (Implemented in Java, runs inside JVM), ***IronRuby*** (Implemented in C#, runs inside .NET framework), ***Rubinius*** (Written in C++ and Ruby) and many more. In this book, we will stick to MRI.

2. Scope

A wide variety of things can be done using Ruby. This is the beauty of being a general purpose programming language. It is possible to build desktop applications, web applications, web services, etc. with Ruby. In fact, Ruby is a very powerful language on the web. There is a widely used web framework called ***Ruby on Rails*** which powers thousands of well-known websites such as ***GitHub, Airbnb, ASKfm, fiverr, Kickstarter, SlideShare, etc.***

GUI applications for desktop can also be developed using Ruby with the help of appropriate bindings of GUI frameworks such as ***shoes, gtk2/3, etc.*** Most databases such as ***MySQL, MSSQL, SQLite, PostgreSQL, etc.*** are supported by Ruby.

Ruby projects can be easily extended using packages called as ***gems***. The official package manager is known as ***RubyGems*** which hosts thousands of gems.

2.1 Prerequisites

Even if you have no programming background, you should have no problems in learning basic Ruby. However, you should be comfortable with using your computer and be well versed with using ***Shell/Terminal*** on Linux/MAC and ***Command Prompt/ PowerShell*** on Windows. I am not saying that you should be a wizard of any sort but should know the basic commands, be comfortable with file system navigation using Shell, Terminal, Command Prompt or PowerShell. If you have any programming knowledge at all, you will really enjoy learning Ruby. If you have a choice to learn any other programming language before Ruby, I would suggest C or C++.

What will I learn from this Ruby book?

This book will teach you to write simple console applications in Ruby. When you come to the end of this book, you will be able to write Ruby scripts that interacts with the user, interacts with the file system, etc. Although Ruby is very useful on the web, this book does not contain any lessons on web specific development because the prerequisite of that is knowing basic web development using languages such as HTML, CSS, Javascript, etc. Having said that, if you are a web developer or know even the basics of web development using HTML, CSS, Javascript, etc., the basic knowledge of Ruby that you gain from this book should be enough for you to self-learn web development using Ruby.

3. Getting Started

You will need a PC/Laptop with Windows/Linux having a reasonably good hardware configuration or a MAC machine to write and execute Ruby scripts/programs. Ruby scripts can be written using any text editor including Notepad. I suggest ***Notepad++*** (https://notepad-plus-plus.org/). Ruby scripts are plain-text files and carry the extension ***.rb***.

Ruby is an interpreted language and a Ruby interpreter is needed to execute Ruby scripts. We will now see how to get started with Ruby interpreter on different platforms.

3.1 Installing Ruby on Windows

Ruby MRI is the reference implementation of Ruby and can be downloaded from https://www.ruby-lang.org/en/downloads/ or https://rubyinstaller.org/downloads/. Download the installer which includes ***MSYS2-Devkit***. This ***Devkit*** is required to compile ***Ruby Gems*** with ***C-extensions***. This is an advanced topic and there are no examples in this book that deal with compilations of Gems with C-extensions. However, it is good to have the ***Devkit*** installed because should you choose to self-learn advance Ruby concepts, you will have all the tools ready on your system. To give you a context, I have chosen ***Ruby+Devkit 2.6.5-1 (x64)*** installation file. You can choose any version of Ruby, later the better. Once you have the appropriate installation file, execute it to begin the installation process. You will see something like this:

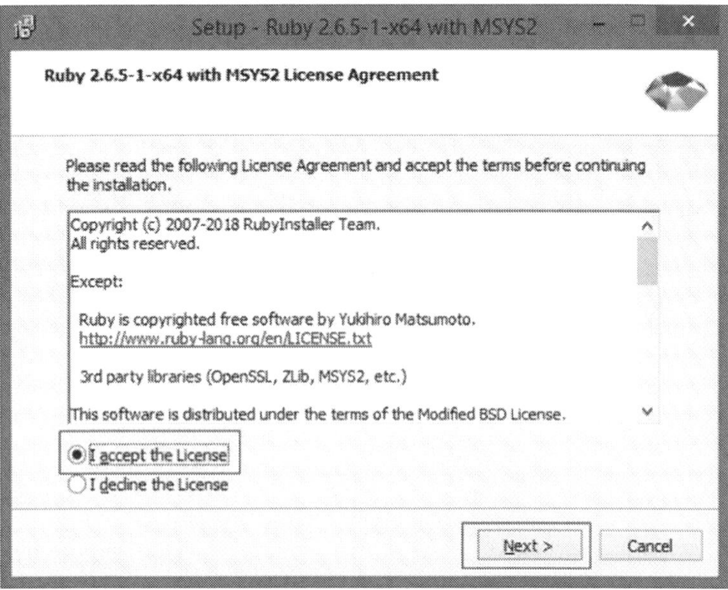

Read the agreement, accept the terms and click ***Next***.

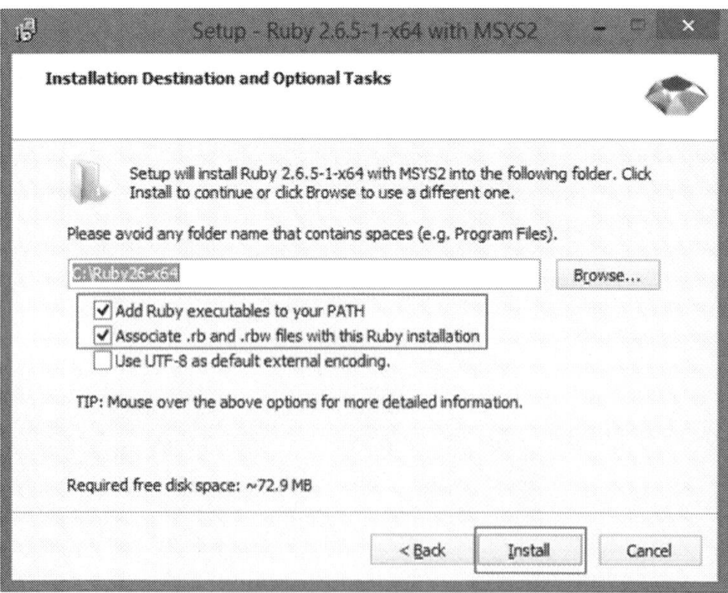

Here, you can choose the directory where the Ruby environment should be installed. It is best to leave it unchanged. Check the options as marked in the image above and hit ***Install***.

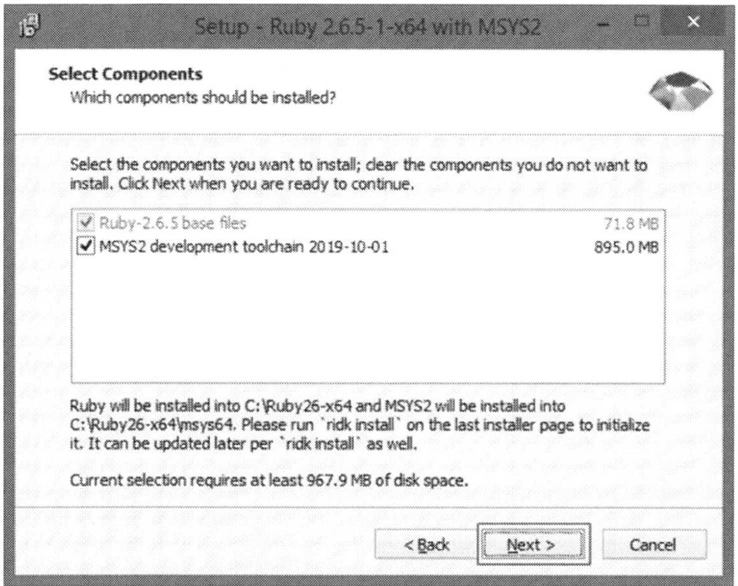

Make sure both the items are checked and click ***Next***.

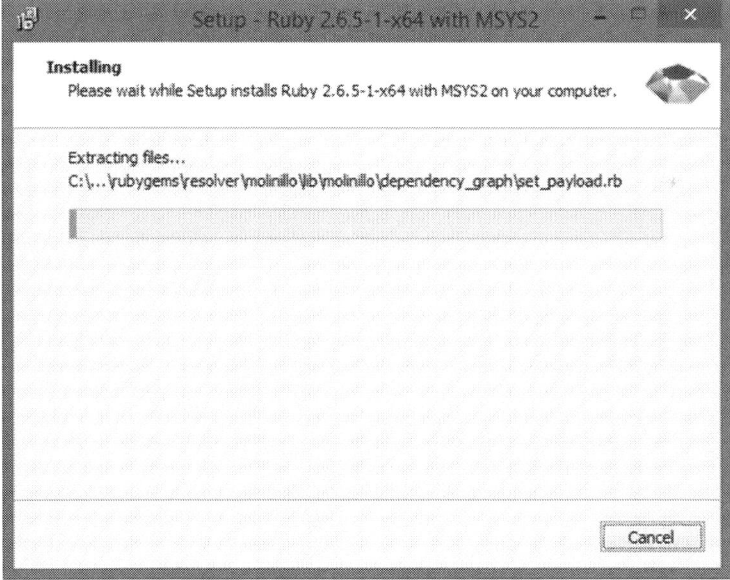

The installation process will now begin and you will see something like this. The whole process may take a few minutes to complete. When it is done, you will see something like this:

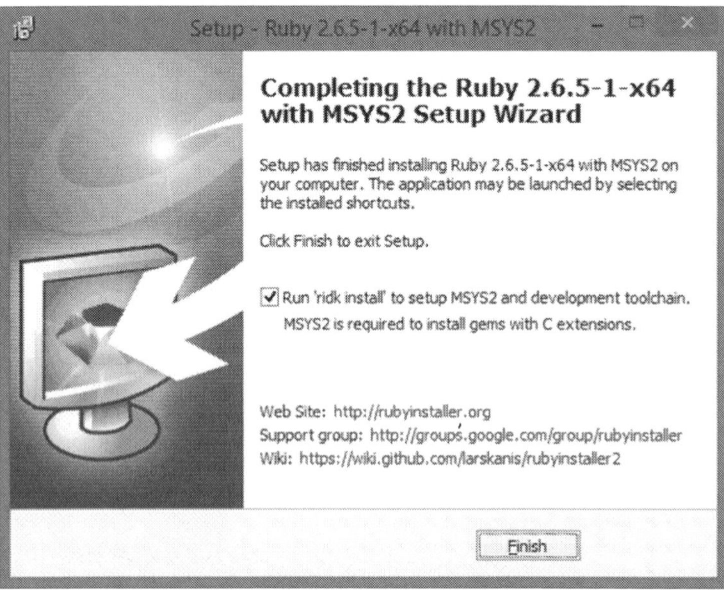

At this point, you will have Ruby environment on your system. Installing ***MSYS2*** is an optional step. You can either do it now or later. If you chose to install it now, check the ***Run 'rdk install'*** option and click ***Finish***. A console application like the one shown in the image below will launch.

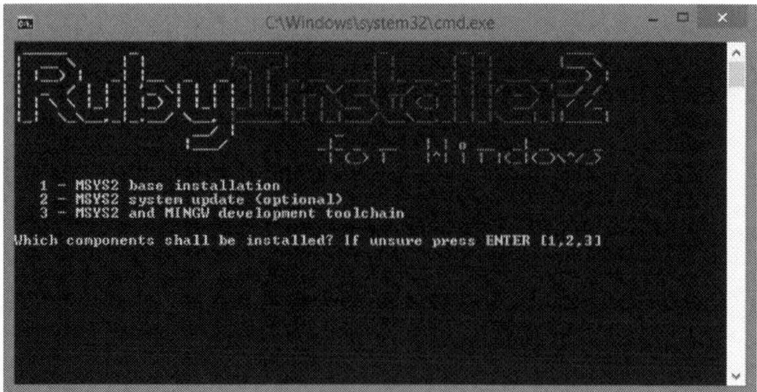

Type 1, press Enter and follow the instruction.

Now that the installation process has finished, let us make sure that the Ruby environment has been set up and ready for use. To do so, open Command Prompt or PowerShell and enter the following command:

ruby -v

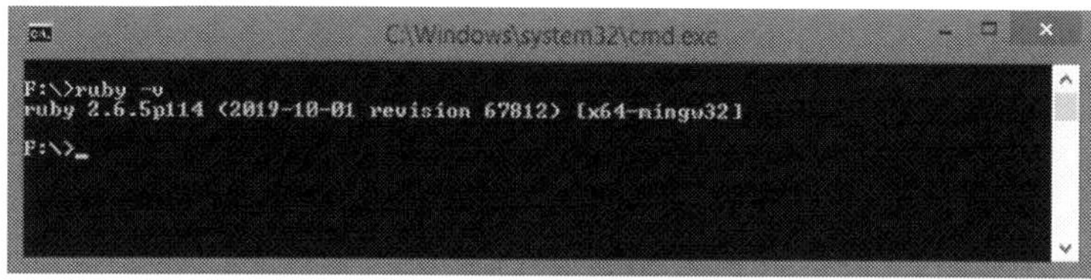

If you see this command return Ruby's version as shown in the image above, it means Ruby has been installed, the environment has been correctly set up and you are good to go!

If you see an error message which looks somewhat like this – ***'ruby' is not recognized as an internal or external command, operable program or batch file.*** Or something similar, it means there is something wrong. In such a case, kindly go through the installation process all over again.

3.2 Installing Ruby on Unix based OS

If you are using Unix based systems such as Linux, BSD (FreeBSD, DragonflyBSD, etc.), macOS, etc., it is most likely that your system already has Ruby environment installed. To check, open Terminal/ Shell and enter the following command:

$>ruby -v

If this command returns the version of Ruby (just like on Windows) as shown in the screenshot below, it means Ruby environment is present and ready for use:

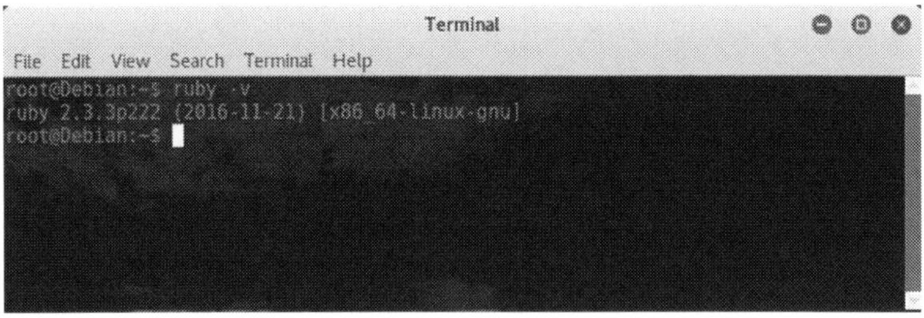

Note: *Ruby version on my machine is an older one but would still do the job. This image is for demonstration purpose only.*

If the Shell/Terminal says command not found or something similar, it means that the Ruby environment is not present and will have to be installed and/or configured. To do so, visit https://www.ruby-lang.org/en/downloads/ and download the appropriate version of Ruby for your operating system.

3.3 Writing Ruby Scripts

A Ruby script is a collection of instructions inside a plain-text file that a Ruby interpreter can understand. As mentioned earlier, Ruby scripts or programs can be written using text editors such as Notepad, Wordpad, vi, emacs, etc. I will be using ***Notepad++***. A script once written should be saved with the extension ***.rb***. This file is referred to as – Ruby program, Ruby script, Ruby source, source code, source file or simply script/program/source.

On Windows, simply open your favourite text editor, write the script and save it as ***<file name>.rb***. On Unix based systems such as Linux, MAC, FreeBSD, etc., you have to do one extra thing – add a ***shebang line***. A shebang line is a sequence of characters beginning with ***#!*** followed by the location of the environment or the script interpreter. In this case, it is the Ruby interpreter. This line should be the first one in your script. The Ruby interpreter is mostly located at ***/usr/bin/ruby***. Hence, on Unix-like systems, the shebang line will look like:

#!/usr/bin/ruby

If you are unsure of the location, you can use ***where*** or ***locate*** commands to determine the exact location of the Ruby interpreter:

$>where ruby

OR

$>locate ruby

On MAC, you can use the ***which*** command:

$>which ruby

These commands will return full path to the Ruby interpreter, simply copy it and use it as a part of your shebang like.

Note: A shebang line is not mandatory but is considered as a good programming practice. Hence, it is recommended that you insert this line in your Ruby scripts on Linux/MAC.

3.4 Executing Ruby Scripts

Ruby scripts can be executed using the ***ruby*** command through Command Prompt/PowerShell on Windows and through Shell/ Terminal on Linux, MAC and other Unix based systems. A general way to use this command for script execution is:

ruby <script name>
Example:
ruby myscript.rb

The ***<script name>*** mentioned in the above syntax is a command line argument that is passed to this command. Let us now get a hands on experience with Ruby script execution on Windows and Unix-like systems.

3.4.1 Ruby Script Execution on Windows

When we say ***ruby*** command on Windows, we refer to the Ruby interpreter ***ruby.exe*** which is located inside the Ruby environment's installation directory. If you did not change the installation directory, it will be most likely ***C:\Ruby<version>\bin***. In order to execute a Ruby script on Windows, open Command Prompt or PowerShell, navigate to the directory where the script is present and run the following command:

```
ruby <script name>
        #OR
ruby.exe <script name>
Example:
ruby myscript.rb
        #OR
ruby.exe myscript.rb
```

3.4.2 Ruby Script Execution on Unix-like OS

On Linux, MAC, FreeBSD and other Unix based operating systems, there are two methods of executing a Ruby script. The first one is fairly straight forward, simply run the ***ruby*** command and supply the script name as an argument. When we say ***ruby*** command on Unix based operating systems, we refer to the Ruby interpreter's binary which is usually located at ***/usr/bin/ruby***. In order to execute a Ruby script on Unix based systems, open Shell

/Terminal, navigate to the directory where the script is present and run the following command:

ruby <script name>
#OR
/usr/bin/ruby <script name>
Example:
ruby myscript.rb
#OR
/usr/bin/ruby myscript.rb

There is another method where you make the Ruby script itself executable. To do so, the script in question must be given executable permissions. The best way to do it is use the ***+x*** option with the ***chmod*** command as follows:

chmod +x <script 1>, <script 2>, ... <script n>
Example:
chmod +x myscript.rb

Once execute permission is given, the script can be executed as follows:

./<script name>
./myscript.rb

Note: This method requires you to have the correct shebang line. The shebang line specifies which interpreter/environment to use to execute the script. If you do not use a shebang line or use an incorrect path, the correct interpreter/environment will not be invoked and your script will fail to execute.

3.5 First Ruby Program

It is time to get hands-on experience with script execution. Open the text editor of your choice, copy and paste the following code. You do not have to understand the specifics of the script right now; all you have to in this section is to learn how to execute a Ruby script.

```
#This is our first ruby program.
#Just a test, only to learn how to execute a Ruby script.

puts "\nThis is our first Ruby script.\nIf you see this, so far so good!\n";
```

Save this script as ***firstscript.rb***.

3.5.1 Execute on Windows

Open Command Prompt or PowerShell and navigate to the directory where you have just saved ***firstcript.rb*** and execute the following command:

ruby firstscript.rb

Here is what you should see:

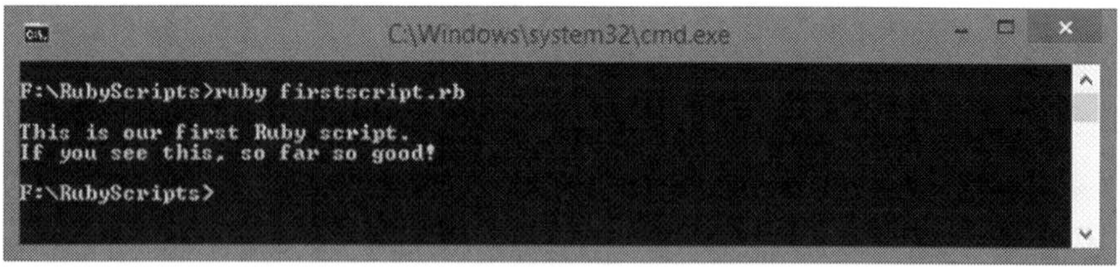

```
C:\Windows\system32\cmd.exe
F:\RubyScripts>ruby firstscript.rb

This is our first Ruby script.
If you see this, so far so good!

F:\RubyScripts>
```

3.5.2 Execute on Unix based OS

On Linux, MAC and other Unix-like systems, modify the above code, add a shebang line pointing to the correct Ruby interpreter and save it as ***firstscript.rb***. The modified code would look somewhat like this:

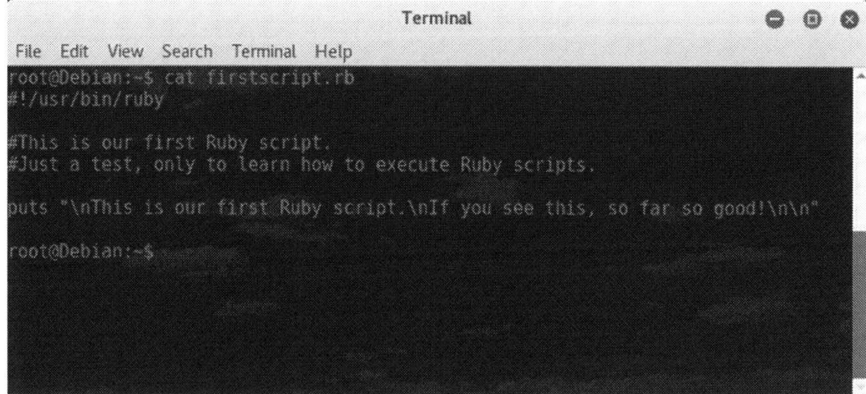

Open Shell/Terminal, navigate to the directory where ***firstscript.rb*** is present and execute the following command:

ruby firstscript.rb

Here is what you should see inside the Terminal/Shell:

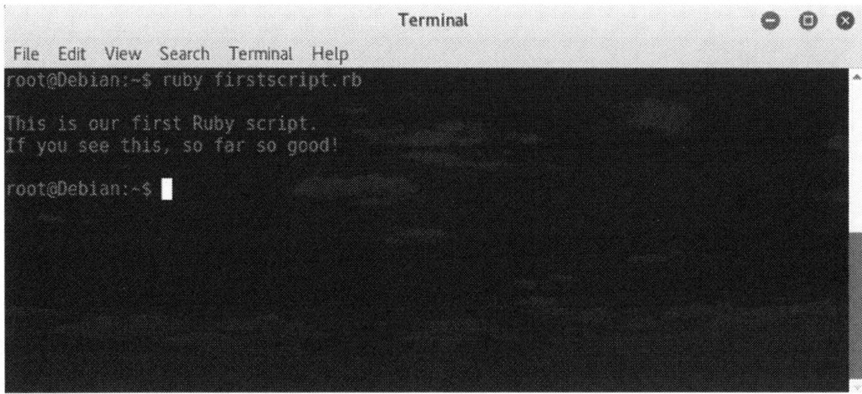

Let us now try the second method of execution where we will make ***firstscript.rb*** executable. To do this, use the following command:

chmod +x firstscript.rb

Execute the script as follows:

./firstscript.rb

You should see something like this:

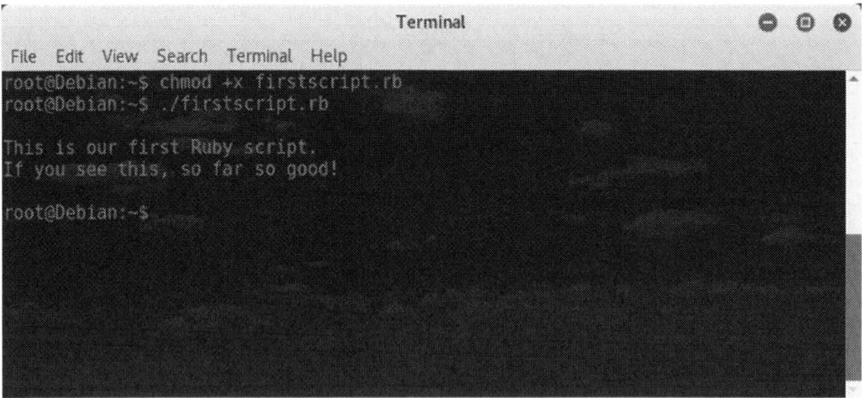

Note: As seen, there is not much of a difference between executing a Ruby script on Windows and executing a Ruby script on Unix based operating systems. For a beginner, it does not matter which OS or text editor you use. It is best to stick to the OS/tools that you are most comfortable with. In this book, all the scripts have been executed on Windows using Command Prompt. The same scripts will work on Linux, MAC, FreeBSD, etc. without any problems unless specified otherwise.

4. Ruby Programming Basics

In this chapter, we will begin with the basics of Ruby programming. Before going ahead, you should be comfortable with your text editor and be able to execute Ruby scripts as demonstrated in the previous chapter. We will make use of ***functions*** or ***methods*** in our scripts. A function/method is a name given to reusable code that can be called to perform various tasks. For example, there is a function to print text into the console, a function to accept input from the user, etc. There is a dedicated chapter on Functions/Methods later in this chapter. Until you get there, you just have to understand what a function is and how to use it.

4.1 Basic Syntax

Ruby is a case sensitive language. This means, the words "Ruby" and "ruby" are treated differently although they may mean the same to us.

4.1.1 Statements

A statement is an instruction or a group of instructions that performs certain operations. This can be anything such as printing some text on the console, compute the product of two numbers, read from a file, etc. In Ruby, a statement ends with a new-line character. This means, while writing Ruby scripts you have to place only one statement on one line. Technically, you can have as many statements as you want on a single line, each one of them separated using a ***semi-colon (;)***. But it is best to avoid doing so. Here are a few examples of valid statements in Ruby:

```
puts 'Enter your name: "
name = gets
a = 6
b = 7
sum = a + b
puts sum
```

4.1.2 Comments

Comments are ignored by the interpreter and have no outcome on the execution of a program. There is no specific rule of when and why to use comments but they provide a convenient option to mark or explain your code. Ruby supports single line comments as well as multi-line comments. Single line comments begin with a ***hash sign (#)***. Here are a few examples:

```
#This is a comment, ignored by the interpreter.
A = 30 #This is also a comment, only this part is ignored by the interpreter.
```

Multi-line comments begin with ***=begin*** and end with ***=end*** and can span over multiple lines. Here is an example:

```
=begin
This is the beginning of the multi-line comment section.
You can have a whole paragraph enclosed here.
Can write as much as you want.
The following line signifies the end of the multi-line comment section.
=end
```

4.1.3 Code block

A block of code is one or more lines of code enclosed within curly brackets or marked by the ***end*** keyword (beginning of the block could be anything such as if, while, etc.). This concept is especially useful when working with decision making, loops, functions/ methods, etc. Here is an example of a code block:

```
while (j < 10) do
        puts j
        j = j + 1
end
```

4.1.4 Identifiers

Identifiers are names given to variables, classes, objects, functions, etc. Identifiers can contain alphanumeric characters and underscore but cannot begin with a number. Also, no other special characters are allowed except for underscore.

4.1.5 Keywords

Keywords are reserved words that cannot be used as identifier names. There are a lot of keywords available in Ruby. Knowing each and every keyword is not needed, more information will be provided about a particular keyword as and when required. Here is a list of keywords and their brief explanation.

__ENCODING__

The script encoding of the current file.

__LINE__

The line number of this keyword in the current file.

__FILE__

The path to the current file.

BEGIN

Runs before any other code in the current file.

END

Runs after any other code in the current file.

alias

Creates an alias between two methods (and other things).

and

Short-circuit Boolean and with lower precedence than &&

begin

Starts an exception handling block.

break

Leaves a block early.

case

Starts a case expression.

class

Creates or opens a class.

def

Defines a method.

defined?

Returns a string describing its argument.

do

Starts a block.

else

The unhandled condition in case, if and unless expressions.

elsif

An alternate condition for an if expression.

end

The end of a syntax block. Used by classes, modules, methods, exception handling and control expressions.

ensure

Starts a section of code that is always run when an exception is raised.

false

Boolean false.

for

A loop that is similar to using the each method.

if

Used for if and modifier if expressions.

in

Used to separate the iterable object and iterator variable in a for loop.

module

Creates or opens a module.

next

Skips the rest of the block.

nil

A false value usually indicating "no value" or "unknown".

not

Inverts the following Boolean expression. Has a lower precedence than!

or

Boolean or with lower precedence than ||

redo

Restarts execution in the current block.

rescue

Starts an exception section of code in a begin block.

retry

Retries an exception block.

return

Exits a method.

self

The object the current method is attached to.

super

Calls the current method in a superclass.

then

Indicates the end of conditional blocks in control structures.

true

Boolean true.

undef

Prevents a class or module from responding to a method call.

unless

Used for unless and modifier unless expressions.

until

Creates a loop that executes until the condition is true.

when

A condition in a case expression.

while

Creates a loop that executes while the condition is true.

yield

Starts execution of the block sent to the current method.

Again, important keywords will be covered as and when the need arises. For reference, use this link https://docs.ruby-lang.org/en/2.2.0/keywords_rdoc.html.

4.2 Hello World! Ruby script

We have studied how to save and execute a Ruby script. In this section, we will learn to write a script that prints something on the console. There are several ways to do this, the easiest option is to use the ***puts*** function. A simple syntax of using this function is as follows:

puts <string>
puts "This should work"
puts 'This should also work!'

As seen from the syntax, the ***puts*** function should be given a string. A string is a sequence of characters enclosed within single or double quotes (there is a whole chapter on strings in this book). There are more useful features of this function, we will learn about them as the need arises. Let us write a script to print Hello World! on the console:

```
#Hello World! Ruby Script
#Makes use of the puts function in the simplest way

puts "Hello World!"
```

I have saved the program as ***helloword.rb*** and run it as ***ruby helloworld.rb***.

<u>Output:</u>

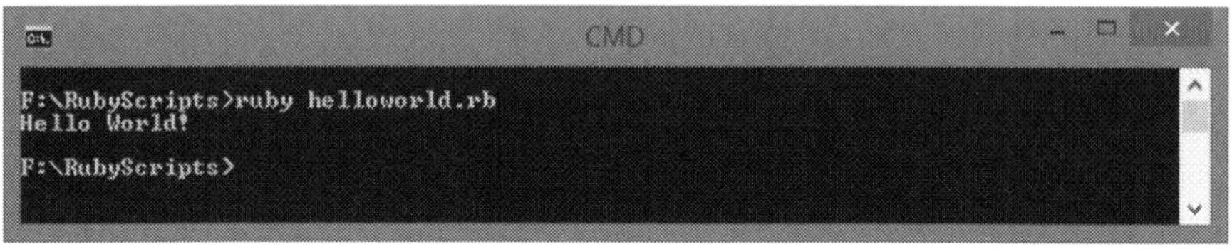

```
CMD
F:\RubyScripts>ruby helloworld.rb
Hello World!

F:\RubyScripts>
```

The escape character in Ruby is ***backslash*** *(\\)*. There are various escape character sequences formed with the help of backslash. Some of the useful ones are ***\n*** and ***\t*** – ***\n*** is the ***newline character***, used to leave a line and ***\t*** is used to leave one ***tab-space***.

4.3 Syntax Error

When you do not follow syntax, the interpreter may return an error. Sometimes, the error message will tell you what is wrong and where; while sometimes the error message can be a little more generic or can have too many details. Let us modify the above script and not enclose ***Hello World!*** within quotes on purpose only to demonstrate how error reporting works:

```
#THIS SCRIPT HAS A SYNTAX ERROR
#ONLY FOR DEMONSTRATION PURPOSE

puts Hello World!
```

Output:

```
CMD
F:\RubyScripts>ruby helloworld.rb
Traceback (most recent call last):
helloworld.rb:4:in `<main>': undefined method `World!' for main:Object (NoMethod
Error)

F:\RubyScripts>
```

In this particular situation, you do know that the error is on line number 4 (*helloworld.rb:4*) but as a beginner, you will not be able to tell what exactly has gone wrong. Hence it is recommended that you stick to the syntax and verify your script before running.

5. Variables

A variable is a name given to a memory location which is used to store data. Every memory location can be accessed using its memory address. Usually, memory addresses are in hexadecimal format. The concept of variables comes in very handy here as it would be difficult to remember hexadecimal addresses as opposed to remembering a meaningful name to given to a memory location. Every variable has a data type. A data type is a category which specifies the type of data we are dealing with. Ruby supports three basic data types – integers, floats and strings.

5.1 Variable Initialization

Explicit declaration of a variable is not required. Variables can be created on the fly directly by assigning values to them. General syntax:

<variable name> = <initial value>

Example:

number = 45.7

count = 25

name = 'Earl'

5.2 Printing Variables

Values of variables can be displayed on the console using the ***puts*** function. General syntax:

puts "#{ <variable> }"

Example:

name = 'Bobby'

age = 43

puts "Name: #{ name } Age: #{ age }"

Here is a demo script on variables:

```
#Variables Demo
#Initialize a few variables
first_name = 'Ally'
last_name = 'Styne'
age = 26
country = "South Africa"
#Print variables
puts "\nFull Name: #{ first_name } #{ last_name }"
puts "\nAge: #{ age } "
puts "\nCountry: #{ country } \n"
```

<u>Output:</u>

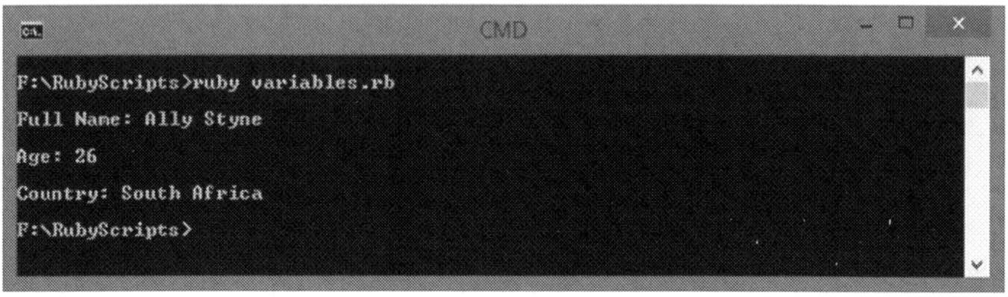

```
CMD
F:\RubyScripts>ruby variables.rb
Full Name: Ally Styne
Age: 26
Country: South Africa
F:\RubyScripts>
```

5.3 Basic Variable Data Types

Here are the basic data types that Ruby supports:

5.3.1 Numbers (Integers and Floats)

Integers and floats are supported in the following formats – signed and unsigned decimal numbers, binary, octal, hexadecimal, floating point values, scientific notations. Here are a few examples:

#Signed integer

a = 653

#Unsigned integer

b = -764

#Simple float

c = 46.73

#Another float

d = -656.352

Binary

x = 0b1011001

#Octal, starts with 0

e = 0153

#Hexadecimal, starts with 0x

f = 0xff

#Scientific notation equivalent to 6.8 x 10^9

g = 6.8E9

5.3.2 Strings

A string is a sequence of characters enclosed either within single quotes or within double quotes. A string cannot start with double quotes and end with a single quote or vice-versa. Here are a few examples of strings:

City = 'Toronto'

Country = "Canada"

The escape character in Ruby is ***backslash (\)*** which is used to include restricted characters within a string. For example, backslash itself is a restricted character because it has some other meaning. On Windows, file paths use backslash to mark a directory. Say, you want to store file path ***D:\notes\ruby.txt*** as string in a variable. You can either enclose this within single quotes like this – ***'D:\notes \ruby.txt'*** and it will work fine or you can enclose it within double quotes and escape each backslash using another backslash like this – ***"D:\\notes\\ruby.txt"***.

5.4 Global Variables

Global variables are those which are accessible from everywhere and their value will be common. Here is how you can initialize a global variable:

$<variable name> = <initial value>
Example:
$flag = 0
$dir = "/home/user1/all.txt"

Note: Apart from global variables, there are more types of variables such as ***instance variables*** and ***class variables***. These concepts will be clearer when appropriate chapters are covered.

6. Introduction to Object Oriented Programming

Ruby supports multiple paradigms; one of them is ***Object Oriented Programming*** (abbreviated as ***OOP***). In this paradigm of programming, emphasis is more on the data and less on the procedure. Object oriented programming is a huge field and covering all concepts is beyond the scope of this book. This chapter will give you a generic introduction to OOP. There is another chapter towards the end of this book called **Introduction to Classes and Objects** which deals with the programming part of OOP and can be treated as an extension of this chapter. When learning object oriented concepts, you should know about two important things – ***classes*** and ***objects***. Of course, learning OOP goes way beyond just learning classes and objects but this is the foundation.

A ***class*** is a user defined data type which contains a collection of variables called ***data members*** and methods known as ***member functions*** used to work on the variables. Data members are also known as ***properties*** or ***attributes***.

An ***object*** is an instance of a class which has <u>its own set of data members</u> as defined in its class. A class is merely a definition and may or may not contain data by itself whereas, an object contains data. Some data members can be shared across all objects; such variables are known as ***class variables*** or ***static variables***. Similarly, some functions can be shared by all objects; such functions are called ***class functions*** or ***static functions***. Let us understand the concept of classes and objects using an example. Consider the following diagram:

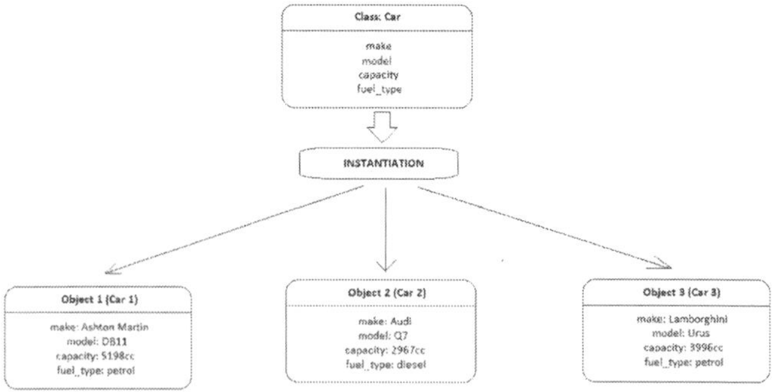

There is a class called ***Car***. The definition of this car contains four data members – ***make, model, capacity and fuel_type***. These data members will be used to store attributes of individual cars. As mentioned earlier, an object is an instance of a class. Three objects are created – ***Object 1, Object 2*** and ***Object 3*** using a process called as ***instantiation***. Each object has its own copy of data members as defined in the ***Car class – make, model, capacity and fuel_type***. Each object can be referred to as an individual car.

As seen in the diagram, objects are used to store data. Although it is possible to store data in the class itself which is also useful in some situations, storing data using objects makes a lot of sense.

6.1 Accessing Data Members/Member functions

Data members and member functions of a class or an object can be accessed using the ***dot (.) operator***. General syntax:

<Object/Class >.<Data Member/Member Function>

Eg:

Math.sin(3.14)

#Math is a class and sin is a static member function of the Math class.

A class can be defined inside another class. This process is called nesting of classes. In order to access the inner classes, you will have to use multiple dot operators in one statement.

7. Operators

An operator is a symbol or a set of symbols used to perform an operation. An operation could be anything like addition, subtraction, comparison of two variables, etc. Ruby offers arithmetic operators, assignment operators, comparison operators, logical operators and bitwise operators. We will take a look at each of these categories with programming examples.

7.1 Arithmetic Operators

Arithmetic operators as the name says are used to perform arithmetic operations such as addition, subtraction, multiplication, etc. Here is a list of all the arithmetic operators:

Operator	Description	Sample Usage	Explanation
+	Addition	x + y	Adds all the operands and returns the arithmetic sum.
-	Subtraction	x - y	Subtracts the operand on the right from the operand on the left, returns the difference.
*	Multiplication	x * y	Multiplies operands and returns the product.
/	Division	x / y	Divides the operand on the left by the operand on the right and returns the quotient. ***Note:*** If you try to divide an integer by another, even if the quotient is a float, only the integer part will be returned.
%	Modulus	x % y	Divides the operand on the left by the operand on the right and returns the remainder.
**	Exponent	x ** y	Raises the power of the operand on the left by a value specified by the operand on the right. Eg. 2 ** 3 is equivalent to 2^3 in mathematical form which is equal to 8.

Multiple operators can also be used in one expression. For example:

*x = a + b *c – (d ** z)*

In such a case, the expression will be evaluated according to mathematical rules. Also, the result of an expression can be directly displayed using ***puts*** function as follows:

puts "#{ <expression> }"

Example:

*puts "#{ a + b * c }"*

Here is a ruby script that demonstrates the usage of arithmetic operators:

```
#Arithmetic operators demo
#Initialize some variables
a = 33
b = -2.7
c = 5.73
d = 14
x = 4
y = 3.4E-03
#Print all variables
puts "\na = #{ a } b = #{ b } c = #{ c } d = #{ d }"
puts "\nx = #{ x } y = #{ y }"
sum = a + x
diff = x - c
prod = b * y
quo = a / x
mod = d % x
exp = x ** y
#Print everything
puts "\na + x = #{ sum } \nx - c = #{ diff } \nb * y =
#{ prod } \na / x (integer) = #{ quo } \na / x (float)
= #{ a / (x * 1.0) }"
puts "d % x = #{ mod } \nx ** y = #{ exp }\n"
```

Output:

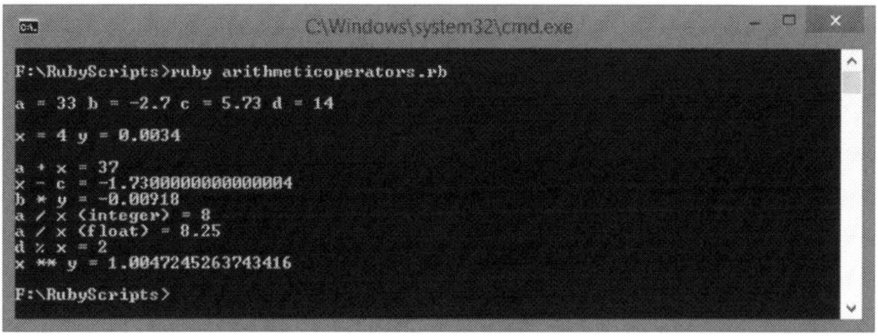

```
C:\Windows\system32\cmd.exe
F:\RubyScripts>ruby arithmeticoperators.rb
a = 33 b = -2.7 c = 5.73 d = 14
x = 4 y = 0.0034
a + x = 37
x - c = -1.7300000000000004
b * y = -0.00918
a / x (integer) = 8
a / x (float) = 8.25
d % x = 2
x ** y = 1.0047245263743416
F:\RubyScripts>
```

7.2 Assignment Operators

Assignment operators are used to assign values to variables. We have seen the basic assignment operator given by the ***equal to (=)*** sign. Here are a few examples:

id = 435

num = 0xfa

word = "Ruby"

It is also possible to assign values to different variables using parallel assignment. General syntax:

<variable 1>, <variable 2>, … <variable n> = <value 1>, <value 2>, … <value n>

Example:

a, b, c = 6, "book", 4.76

In the above example, ***a*** will have the value ***6***, ***b*** will have the value ***"book"*** and ***c*** will have the value ***4.76***.

Operator	Description	Sample Usage	Equivalent To	Explanation
+=	Add and Assign	x += y	x = x + y	Computes the arithmetic sum of the given operands and assigns the resulting value to the operand on the left.
-=	Subtract and Assign	x -= y	x = x – y	Computes the arithmetic difference of the given operands and assigns the resulting value to the operand on the left.
*=	Multiply and Assign	x *= y	x = x * y	Multiplies the given operands and assigns the product to the operand on the left.
/=	Divide and Assign	x /= y	x = x / y	Divides the given operands and assigns the quotient to the operand on the left.
%=	Take Modulus and Assign	x %= y	x = x % y	Divides the given operands and assigns the remainder to the operand on the left.
**=	Raise power and Assign	x **= y	x = x ** y	Raises the power of the operand on the left by a value of the operand on the right and assigns the resulting value to the operand on the left.

Here is a Ruby script that demonstrates the working of assignment operators:

```
#Assignment operators demo
#Initialize some variables
a, b, c, d = 4, 7, -1.78, 11
x = 3
y = -1.2E1
#Print all variables
```

```
puts "\na = #{ a } b = #{ b } c = #{ c } d = #{ d }"
puts "\nx = #{ x } y = #{ y }"
#Perform compound assignment operations
a += b
c -= d
b *= d
d %= x
x **= y
y /= 6.74
#Print everything
puts "\na += b : #{ a } \nc -= d : #{ c } \nb *= d : #{
b } \nd %= x : #{ d } \nx **= y : #{ x }"
puts "y /= 6.74 : #{ y } \n"
```

Output:

```
F:\RubyScripts>ruby assignmentoperators.rb

a = 4 b = 7 c = -1.78 d = 11

x = 3 y = -12.0

a += b : 11
c -= d : -12.78
b *= d : 77
d %= x : 2
x **= y : 1.8816764231589208e-06
y /= 6.74 : -1.7804154302670623

F:\RubyScripts>_
```

7.3 Comparison Operators

Comparison operators are used to compare more than one variables, values or expressions. For example, using these operators whether the value of a variable is equal to another one, whether a variable is less than another one and so on. The result of such operations is either ***true*** or ***false*** in most cases. These operators are heavily used in control structures.

Operator	Description	Sample Usage	Explanation
==	Equal To	x == y	Returns **true** if the values of all the operands are equal, returns **false** otherwise.
!=	Not Equal To	x != y	Returns **true** if the values of the operands are not equal, returns **false** otherwise.
<	Less Than	x < y	Returns **true** if the value of the operand on the left is less than the value of the operand on the right, returns **false** otherwise.
>	Greater Than	x > y	Returns **true** if the value of the left operand is greater than the value of the operand on the right, returns **false** otherwise.
<=	Less Than OR Equal To	x <= y	Returns **true** if the value of the left operand is less than ***OR equal to*** the value of the operand on the right, returns **false** otherwise.
>=	Greater Than OR Equal To	x >= y	Returns **true** if the value of the left operand is greater than ***OR equal to*** the value of the operand on the right, returns **false** otherwise.
<=>	Combined Comparison Operator	x <=> y	Returns *-1* if x is less than y, returns *0* if x is equal to y and returns *1* if x is greater than y.

Here is a script that uses all these operators:

```
#Comparison Operators
#Initialize 2 variables
x, y = 50, 10
#Print x and y
puts "\nx = #{ x } y = #{ y }"
#Print comparison results
puts "\nx > y: #{ x > y } \nx < y: #{ x < y } \nx == y:
#{ x == y } \nx != y: #{ x != y } \nx >= y: #{ x >= y }
\nx <= y: #{ x <= y } \nx <=> y: #{ x <=> y }\n"
```

Output:

```
F:\RubyScripts>ruby comparisonoperators.rb
x = 50 y = 10
x > y: true
x < y: false
x == y: false
x != y: true
x >= y: true
x <= y: false
x <=> y: 1
F:\RubyScripts>
```

7.4 Logical Operators

Logical operators perform logical operations such as ***and***, ***or*** and ***not*** on the given operands. Operands are usually Boolean expressions which evaluate to ***true*** or ***false***.

Operator (s)	Description	Sample Usage	Explanation
or ||	Logical OR	(x or y) (x || y)	Compares operands and returns ***true*** if any one of the values is True, returns ***false*** only if all the operands are false .
and &&	Logical AND	(x and y) (x && y)	Compares operands and returns ***true*** if all the values are True, returns ***false*** if any one of the expressions evaluate to false.
not !	Logical NOT	not x !x	Inverts the Boolean value – not True will return ***false*** and not False will return ***true***.

Here is a script that demonstrates the usage of logical operators:

```
#Logical Operators
#Initialize 2 variables
x, y = -15, 32
#Print x and y
puts "\nx = #{ x } y = #{ y }"
#Print results
puts "\n(x < 0) && (x < y): #{ (x < 0) && (x < y) }"
puts "\n(x > 0) and (x == y): #{ (x > 0) and (x == y) }"
puts "\n(x != y) || (x > y): #{ (x != y) || (x > y) }"
puts "\n(y < 0) or (y > x): #{ (y < 0) or (y > x) }"
puts "\nnot (x == -15): #{ not (x == -15) }"
puts "\n!(y == 0): #{ !(y == 0) }"
```

Output:

```
C:\Windows\system32\cmd.exe
F:\RubyScripts>ruby logicaloperators.rb
x = -15 y = 32
(x < 0) && (x < y): true
(x > 0) and (x == y): false
(x != y) || (x > y): true
(y < 0) or (y > x): true
not (x == -15): false
!(y == 0): true
F:\RubyScripts>
```

7.5 Bitwise Operators

Bitwise operators perform operations on operands in a bit by bit manner. In order to understand this class of operators, you need to have basic knowledge of the binary number system and/or Boolean algebra.

<table>
<tr><th>Operator</th><th>Description</th><th>Sample Usage</th><th>Explanation</th></tr>
<tr><td>|</td><td>Bitwise OR</td><td>x | y</td><td>Performs Logical OR on each of the bits of the operands.</td></tr>
<tr><td>&</td><td>Bitwise AND</td><td>x & y</td><td>Performs Logical AND on each of the bits of the operands.</td></tr>
<tr><td>^</td><td>Bitwise XOR</td><td>x ^ y</td><td>Performs Logical XOR on each of the bits of the operands.</td></tr>
<tr><td>~</td><td>One's Complement</td><td>~x</td><td>Calculate one's complement of the given operand.</td></tr>
<tr><td><<</td><td>Left Shift</td><td>x << y</td><td>Left shift the bits of the operand on the left by a number of times specified by the value of the operand on the right. For example, x << 5 means left shift the bits of x, 5 times.</td></tr>
<tr><td>>></td><td>Right Shift</td><td>x >> y</td><td>Right shift the bits of the operand on the left by a number of times specified by the value of the operand on the right. For example, x >> 2 means right shift the bits of x, 2 times.</td></tr>
</table>

In order to demonstrate the working of bitwise operators, we need to be able to see the binary equivalent of a number. To do so, we will be using the ***to_s(<base>)*** function. This function converts a given number to a string according to the specified ***<base>***. Base refers to the base of the number system to be converted to. For example, for ***binary number system***, the base is *2*, for ***octal*** it is *8* and for ***hexadecimal***, it is *16*. The ***to_s(<base>)*** function converts the given number to the specified base and returns it in string format. You can either use a variable to receive it or directly print the value using puts function. General syntax:

<variable>.to_s(<base>)

Example:

x = 4

x_binary = x.to_s(2)

puts "#{ x } in binary is # { x.to_s(2) }"

Here is a script that demonstrates the usage of bitwise operators:

```
#Bitwise Operators
#Initialize a few variables
a = 16
b = 39
c = 0b10010
d = 0xFC
#Display
puts "\na: #{ a } \t\tbinary: #{ a.to_s(2) }"
puts "\nb: #{ b } \t\tbinary: #{ b.to_s(2) }"
puts "\nc: #{ c } \t\tbinary: #{ c.to_s(2) }"
puts "\nd: #{ d } \t\tbinary: #{ d.to_s(2) }"
p = a | b
q = c & d
r = b ^ c
s = ~b
x = c << 3
y = d >> 5
#Display results of bitwise operations
puts "\na | b : #{ p } \tbinary: #{ p.to_s(2) }"
puts "\nc & d : #{ q } \tbinary: #{ q.to_s(2) }"
puts "\nb ^ c : #{ r } \tbinary: #{ r.to_s(2) }"
puts "\n~b : #{ s } \tbinary: #{ s.to_s(2) }"
puts "\nc << 3 : #{ x } \tbinary: #{ x.to_s(2) }"
puts "\nd >> 5 : #{ y } \tbinary: #{ y.to_s(2) }\n"
```

Output:

```
C:\Windows\system32\cmd.exe

F:\RubyScripts>ruby bitwiseoperators.rb
a: 16           binary: 10000
b: 39           binary: 100111
c: 18           binary: 10010
d: 252          binary: 11111100
a | b : 55      binary: 110111
c & d : 16      binary: 10000
b ^ c : 53      binary: 110101
~b : -40        binary: -101000
c << 3 : 144    binary: 10010000
d >> 5 : 7      binary: 111
F:\RubyScripts>_
```

8. Ruby Shell

Ruby Shell or ***Interactive Ruby Shell*** abbreviated as ***irb*** is an ***REPL*** (read-eval-print-loop) application which is used to interact with the ***Ruby Interpreter***. Generally, REPL applications accept instructions from the user, execute them and print the result inside the shell. Such shells are very useful when it comes to testing and prototyping. In order to start the Ruby Shell, open Command Prompt/PowerShell on Windows or Shell/Terminal on Linux, MAC or other Unix-like operating systems and enter the following command:

irb

The Ruby Shell should look something like this on Windows:

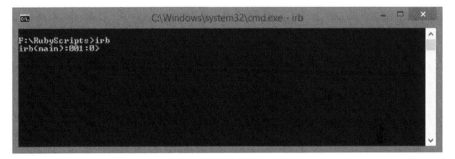

On Linux, it looks something like this:

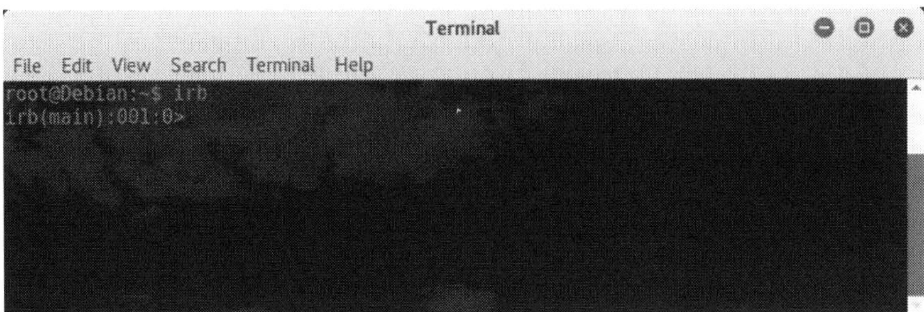

This shell is an interface between the programmer and the Ruby Interpreter. You can enter any Ruby statement, it will be processed and the result will be printed inside the shell right away. Let us enter some Ruby statements based on the concepts that we have learned so far and see what happens. Enter the following statements one by one, feel free to try out some more statements of your own:

```
puts "This is being printed inside the shell!!!"
3 + 5
7 / (3 * 1.0)
a = 6
b = 9
c = -5
d = 2.45E2
a + b
c - d
a * d
d / c
b % b % 22
a > b
c < d
b == c
c != d
a <=> b
a.to_s(2)
app = 'Shell'
puts app
```

Here is the shell output:

```
C:\Windows\system32\cmd.exe - irb
F:\RubyScripts>irb
irb(main):001:0> puts "This is being printed inside the shell!!!"
This is being printed inside the shell!!!
=> nil
irb(main):002:0> 3 + 5
=> 8
irb(main):003:0> 7 / (3 * 1.0)
=> 2.3333333333333335
irb(main):004:0> a = 6
=> 6
irb(main):005:0> b = 9
=> 9
irb(main):006:0> c = -5
=> -5
irb(main):007:0> d = 2.45E2
=> 245.0
irb(main):008:0> a + b
=> 15
irb(main):009:0> c - d
=> -250.0
irb(main):010:0> a * d
=> 1470.0
irb(main):011:0> d / c
=> -49.0
irb(main):012:0> b % 2
=> 1
irb(main):013:0> a > b
=> false
irb(main):014:0> c < d
=> true
irb(main):015:0> b == c
=> false
irb(main):016:0> c != d
=> true
irb(main):017:0> a <=> b
=> -1
irb(main):018:0> a.to_s(2)
=> "110"
irb(main):019:0> app = 'Shell'
=> "Shell"
irb(main):020:0> puts app
Shell
=> nil
irb(main):021:0> _
```

If you want to quit the shell, use ***exit*** or ***quit*** command. The shell will also tell you if there is a syntax error; after all, it is the same Ruby interpreter. Let me commit a syntax error on purpose just to demonstrate what happens. I will try to initialize a string variable without enclosing the string within quotes. Here is what happens:

```
C:\Windows\system32\cmd.exe - irb
F:\RubyScripts>irb
irb(main):001:0> name = Shanon
Traceback (most recent call last):
        4: from C:/Ruby26-x64/bin/irb.cmd:31:in `<main>'
        3: from C:/Ruby26-x64/bin/irb.cmd:31:in `load'
        2: from C:/Ruby26-x64/lib/ruby/gems/2.6.0/gems/irb-1.0.0/exe/irb:11:in `
<top (required)>'
        1: from (irb):1
NameError (uninitialized constant Shanon)
irb(main):002:0>
```

As seen, the Ruby Shell is a very useful tool. When you are learning any Ruby concept, it is recommended that this shell be kept open so that you can try out any new statements that you learn. As the result will be given to you then and there, you will get a better understanding of how the statement actually works. This is a prototyping tool which will help you in understanding how Ruby statements work and you will also be able to test your ideas. This is definitely not a substitute to writing and executing scripts. We will still be writing and executing plenty of scripts in the chapters to follow.

9. User Input

In this chapter, we will learn how to interact with the user. All this while we had been using hardcoded values inside our Ruby scripts. None of the scripts accepted any form of input from the user. To read input from the user, we use a built in method called ***gets***. General Syntax:

<variable> = gets

Example:

name = gets

In short, the ***gets*** function reads the user input and returns it in string format. There must be a variable to receive the returned input. In the above example, ***name*** is the variable which will receive the returned string value. When the Ruby interpreter encounters the ***gets*** statement, the script will halt execution temporarily and wait for the user to enter something through the keyboard (and press Enter). This is a ***blocking I/O operation***; i.e. this system call is blocking the normal flow of execution by waiting for an event to occur which is user input in this case. When the user enters something (and presses Enter), the ***gets*** function does all the heavy lifting (internally) which is required to fetch data from the input stream and eventually returns whatever the user has entered in string format.

Let us write a Ruby script where we will ask the user to enter something, we will read that input using the ***gets*** function, print the same text and its length back. In order to determine the length of a string, we can use the ***length*** method as follows:

<length variable> = <string variable>.length

Example:

len = name.length

Here is the script:

```
#User Input using Prompt
#gets method is used

puts "\nEnter some text and press Enter: \n"
text = gets
puts "\nYou have entered: #{ text } \n\nInput string
length: #{ text.length } "
```

Output:

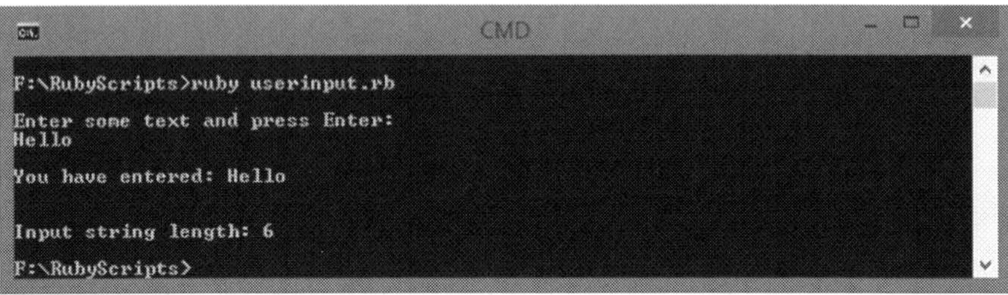

In the above execution, we have entered ***"Hello"*** as the input. The word ***"Hello"*** has 5 characters but our script says it has 6 characters. To see what is going on internally, we turn to the ***Interactive Ruby Shell (irb).*** Open Command Prompt/ PowerShell/Terminal/Sell and enter ***irb*** as instructed in the previous chapter. Enter the following Ruby statement in the shell:

```
text = gets
```

Enter ***"Hello"*** at the prompt and press enter:

```
CMD - irb
F:\RubyScripts>irb
irb(main):001:0> text = gets
Hello
=> "Hello\n"
irb(main):002:0> _
```

Whatever you enter will be printed back. You can enter the variable name (***text***) and press enter to cross check:

```
F:\RubyScripts>irb
irb(main):001:0> text = gets
Hello
=> "Hello\n"
irb(main):002:0> text
=> "Hello\n"
irb(main):003:0> _
```

As seen, our input string ***"Hello"*** gets appended with ***"\n"*** at the end which is the newline character. This happens because, when we enter something through the keyboard, pressing Enter appends the newline character. This is the extra character because of which the input string length was seen to be 6 instead of 5. To solve this problem, we can use the ***chomp*** method to truncate the trailing newline character. General syntax:

<chomped string variable> = <string variable>.chomp

Example:

name = name_input.chomp

Again, there should be a variable to receive the chomped string. Without which, the chomped string will be lost. Let us make use of this function in the previous script:

```
#User Input using Prompt
#gets method is used
#chomp method is used to take out trailing newline
character

puts "Enter some text and press Enter: "
text = gets
text_chomped = text.chomp
puts "\nYou have entered: #{ text_chomped } \n\nInput
string length: #{ text.length } \n\nChomped string
length: #{ text_chomped.length }"
```

Output:

```
F:\RubyScripts>ruby user_input_chomp.rb
Enter some text and press Enter:
Hello

You have entered: Hello

Input string length: 6

Chomped string length: 5

F:\RubyScripts>_
```

Whenever you use ***gets*** function to read user input, always use ***chomp*** function to get rid of the trailing *"\n"* character. Let us write another script to read multiple values from the user, chomp them and print them back:

```
#User Input Extended
#Get multiple values and chomp

puts "Enter your first name: "
first_name = gets
puts "Enter your last name: "
last_name = gets
puts "Enter your age: "
age = gets
puts "Enter your city: "
city = gets
puts "Enter your country: "
country = gets
#Chomp all inputs
first_name = first_name.chomp
last_name = last_name.chomp
age = age.chomp
city = city.chomp
country = country.chomp
#Print everything
puts "You have entered:"
puts "\nFirst Name: #{ first_name } \nLast Name: #{
last_name } \nAge: #{ age } \nCity: #{ city } \nCountry:
#{ country } \n"
```

Output:

```
F:\RubyScripts>ruby userinput_extended.rb
Enter your first name:
Queeney
Enter your last name:
Campbell
Enter your age:
19
Enter your city:
Oklahoma City
Enter your country:
USA
You have entered:

First Name: Queeney
Last Name: Campbell
Age: 19
City: Oklahoma City
Country: USA

F:\RubyScripts>_
```

The ***gets*** function returns the input in string format. Which means, even if the user enters numeric values, they will be considered as strings. This is alright if you want to just display them back but if you want to perform mathematical operations, ***gets*** function alone is not going to be enough. You will have to convert numbers in string format to the appropriate numeric formats. You can use two functions – ***to_i()*** and ***to_f()*** to convert a number from string to integer and float respectively. General syntax:

> *<integer variable> = <number in string>.to_i( )*
>
> *<float variable> = <number in string>.to_f( )*
>
> *Example(s):*
>
> *x = num_str.to_i ( )*
>
> *y = num_str.to_f ( )*

Let us write a Ruby script to add two numbers. We will first read two numbers, chomp the input and convert the numbers in string format to integers:

```
#User Input - Read Integers
#<variable>.to_i() function is used to convert string to
integer

#Prompt the user to enter a number
puts "Enter a number: "
num1_str = gets
num1_str = num1_str.chomp
#Prompt the user to enter another number
puts "Enter another number: "
num2_str = gets
num2_str = num2_str.chomp
#Convert num1_str and num2_str to integer formats
num1 = num1_str.to_i()
num2 = num2_str.to_i()
#Calculate sum
sum = num1 + num2
#Print sum
puts "\nSum: #{ sum }"
```

Output:

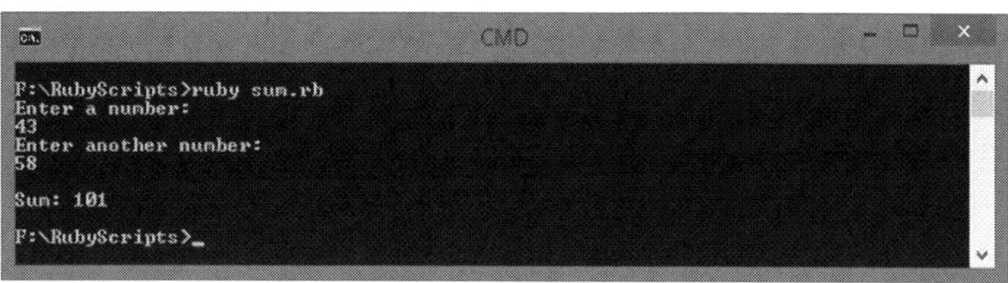

Let us write another Ruby script where we will read two numbers, convert them to float and display their sum, difference, product, quotient and exponential value:

```
#User Input - Read Float
#<variable>.to_f() function is used to convert string to
float

#Prompt the user to enter a number
puts "Enter a number: "
num1_str = gets
num1_str = num1_str.chomp
#Prompt the user to enter another number
puts "Enter another number: "
num2_str = gets
```

```
num2_str = num2_str.chomp
#Convert num1_str and num2_str to float formats
num1 = num1_str.to_f()
num2 = num2_str.to_f()
#Perform arithmetic operations
sum = num1 + num2
diff = num1 - num2
prod = num1 * num2
quo = num1 / num2
exp = num1 ** num2
#Print everything
puts "\nSum: #{ sum } \nDifference: #{ diff } \nProduct:
#{ prod } \nQuotient: #{ quo } \nExp: #{ exp }"
```

Output:

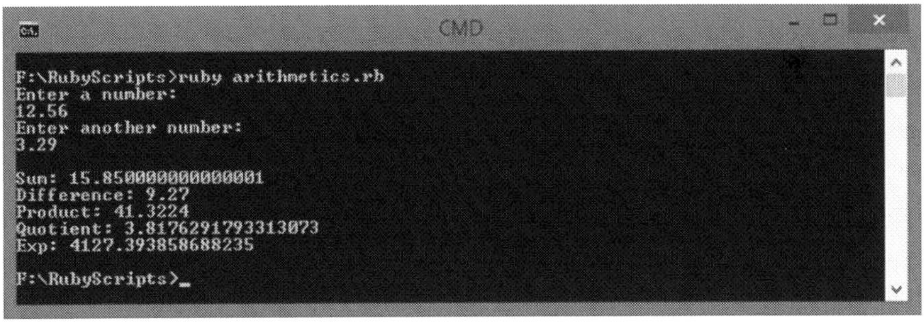

```
CMD
F:\RubyScripts>ruby arithmetics.rb
Enter a number:
12.56
Enter another number:
3.29

Sum: 15.850000000000001
Difference: 9.27
Product: 41.3224
Quotient: 3.8176291793313073
Exp: 4127.393858688235

F:\RubyScripts>_
```

10. Control Structures

Normally, a Ruby script when executed starts executing in a sequential manner starting from the first statement to the last one. This linear execution of a script can be altered with the help of ***Control Structures***. Control structures are programming constructs which help programmers in exercising control over the execution of a script/program by introducing conditionality. Ruby offers control structures in the form of decision making constructs and loops.

10.1 Decision Making

Ruby offers decision making features in the form of ***if-else*** and ***case-when*** constructs.

10.1.1 if-else

The ***if-else*** construct is used to execute a piece of code based on the validity of a condition. The simplest way to use this construct is to use a single ***if-block***. An ***if-block*** begins with an ***if statement*** and ends with the ***end*** keyword. General syntax:

```
if (<condition>)
        #Statements to be executed if <condition> is true.
end
Example:
if (a == 0)
        puts "a is zero"
end
```

An if statement should be given a condition marked by ***<condition>*** in the above code snippet. This condition is usually a Boolean expression which can evaluate to either ***true*** or ***false***. When an if statement is encountered, the given condition is evaluated. If it evaluates to ***true***, the statements inside the ***if-block*** will be executed one by one and if the condition evaluates to ***false***, the block will not be executed. Here is a Ruby script that demonstrates what happens when the given condition of an ***if statement*** evaluates to ***true***:

```
#If demo 1
puts "\nRuby script begins executing."
num = 5
if (num == 5)
      puts "\nIf block activated because num = #{ num }"
      puts "\nCondition of if statement was num == 5 which evaluated to true"
      puts "\nAnother statement under if block"
end
puts "\nRuby script ends here."
```

Output:

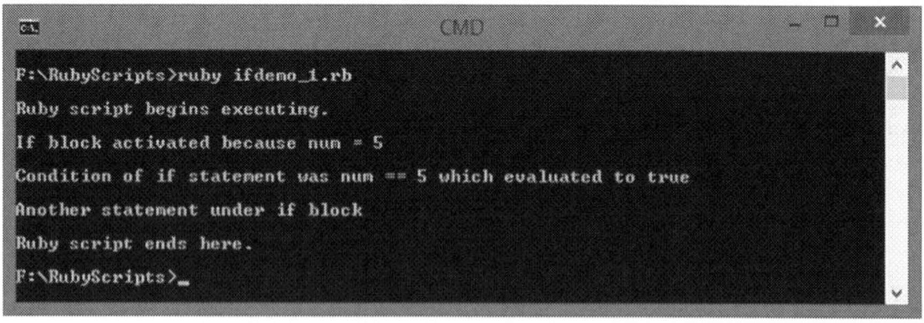

```
F:\RubyScripts>ruby ifdemo_1.rb
Ruby script begins executing.
If block activated because num = 5
Condition of if statement was num == 5 which evaluated to true
Another statement under if block
Ruby script ends here.
F:\RubyScripts>_
```

As seen, the statements under the ***if-block*** are executed one by one. Now, we will edit the code and make sure that the condition evaluates to ***false*** and see what happens:

```
#If demo 2
puts "\nRuby script begins executing."
num = 5
if (num == 10)
      puts "\nIf block activated because num = #{ num }"
      puts "\nCondition of if statement was num == 10"
      puts "\nAnother statement under if block"
end
puts "\nRuby script ends here."
```

Output:

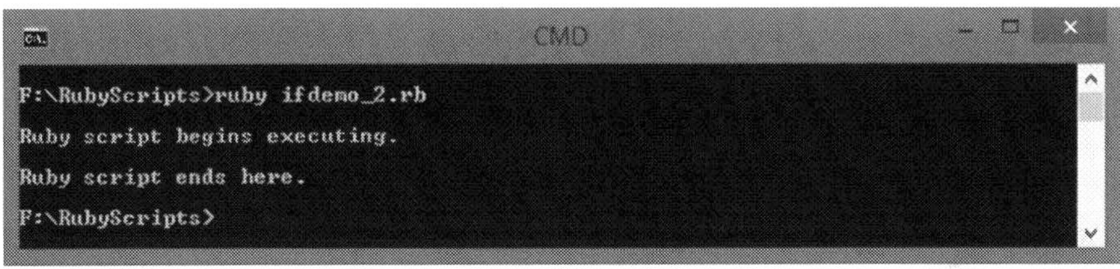

As seen, because the condition evaluates to ***false***, the statements inside the ***if-block*** are not executed. What you see in the console are the statements which are outside the ***if-block***.

This was a simple example, if a condition is ***true***, do something otherwise do nothing. What if we want to do something else when the given condition of the ***if statement*** evaluates to ***false***? For that, we have to use ***else-block***. An ***else-block*** begins with the ***else statement*** and ends with an ***end*** keyword which is common for one set of ***if-else*** blocks. An ***else-block*** cannot exist on its own, it needs a preceding ***if-block***. General syntax:

if (<condition>)

#Statements to be executed if <condition> is true.

else

#Statements to be executed if <condition> is false.

end

Example:

if (a == 0)

puts "a is zero"

else

puts "a is not zero"

end

By now, we know that an ***if-block*** will be executed if the given condition evaluates to ***true***. If the condition evaluates to ***false***, the ***if-block*** will be skipped and the following ***else-block*** (if it is present) will be executed. Here is an example:

```
#If else demo
puts "\nRuby script begins executing."
num = 5
if (num == 10)
      puts "\nIf block activated because num = #{ num }"
      puts "\nCondition of if statement was num == 10"
      puts "\nAnother statement under if block"
else
      puts "\nElse block activated because num = #{ num
}"
      puts "\nCondition of if statement was num == 10
which evaluated to false"
      puts "\nAnother statement under if block"
end
puts "\nRuby script ends here."
```

Output:

```
F:\RubyScripts>ruby ifelsedemo.rb
Ruby script begins executing.
Else block activated because num = 5
Condition of if statement was num == 10 which evaluated to false
Another statement under if block
Ruby script ends here.
F:\RubyScripts>
```

One set of ***if-else*** combination will either execute the ***if-block*** if the given condition is ***true*** or an ***else-block*** if the given condition is ***false***. If you want to check for more conditions, you can nest ***if-else*** blocks within other ***if-else*** blocks. Nested ***if-else*** blocks can further nest more ***if-else*** blocks. Each ***if-else*** block will have its own ***end*** statement to mark the end of that particular block. Any level of nesting is allowed. Let us write A Ruby script where we will ask the user to enter a number and check whether it is positive, negative or zero. Here, we have to account for *three outcomes (positive, negative and zero)*, one ***if-else*** block can only account for *two outcomes (one when the condition is true and the other when the condition is false)*. Hence, we will have to nest ***if-else blocks*** within other ***if-else blocks***:

```
#if else nested demo
#determine if an entered number is +ve, -ve or 0
#Prompt the user to enter a number
puts "\nEnter a number: \n"
num_str = gets
num_str = num_str.chomp
#Convert num_str to integer format
num = num_str.to_i()
#check if num is greater than or equal to 0
if (num >= 0)
      #check if num is greater than 0
      if (num > 0)
            puts "\n#{ num } is positive."
      #if num is greater than or equal to 0 and not
positive, means it is 0
      else
            puts "\n#{ num } is zeo."
      end
#if num is not greater than or equal to zero means it is
negative
else
      puts "\n#{ num } is negative."
end
```

Output:

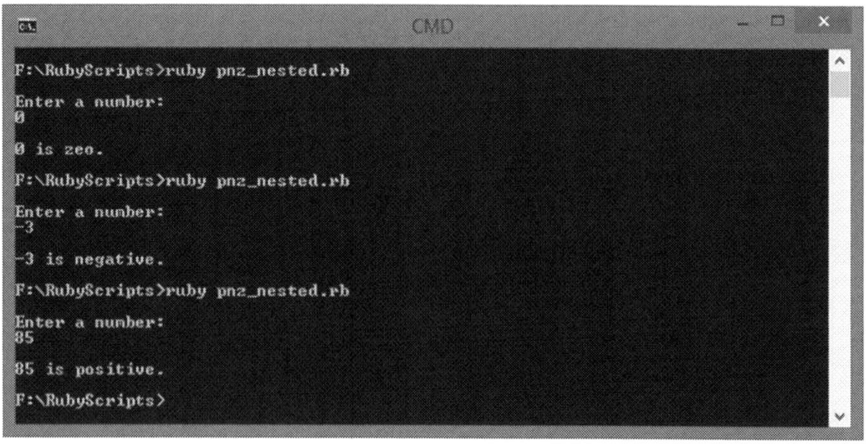

```
F:\RubyScripts>ruby pnz_nested.rb
Enter a number:
0

0 is zeo.
F:\RubyScripts>ruby pnz_nested.rb
Enter a number:
-3

-3 is negative.
F:\RubyScripts>ruby pnz_nested.rb
Enter a number:
85

85 is positive.
F:\RubyScripts>
```

There is another way of checking for more than one conditions without necessarily nesting ***if-else*** blocks. This method involves using the ***elsif*** statement. The ***elsif*** statement has its own condition; it cannot exist on its own and needs a preceding ***if statement***. Multiple ***elsif-blocks*** can be sandwiched between an ***if-block*** and an ***else-block*** with each ***elsif*** statement having its own condition. If the condition of an ***elsif-block*** evaluates to ***true***, that particular ***elsif*** block will be executed. Here is a code snippet that shows how you can check for multiple conditions using multiple ***elsif*** blocks:

if (<condition 1>)

#Statements to be executed if <condition 1> is true

elsif (<condition 2>)

#Statements to be executed if <condition 1> is false and <condition 2> is true

elsif (<condition 3>)

#Statements to be executed if <condition 1> is false and <condition 3> is true …

…

#More elsif blocks can be placed here

…

…

elsif (<condition n>)

#Statements to be executed if <condition 1> is false and <condition n> is true else

#Statements to be executed if all the conditions evaluate to false

end

Here is how ***if-elsif-else*** combination works – When the ***if*** statement is encountered, its condition will be evaluated, if it evaluates to ***true***, statements under the ***if-block*** will be executed one by one. That is, it! End of story! All the following blocks will be skipped. However, if the condition evaluates to ***false***, the execution control will jump to the immediate ***elsif-block*** and its condition will be evaluated. If that condition evaluates to ***true***, that particular ***elsif-block*** will be executed and rest of the blocks will be skipped. If the condition of an ***elsif-block*** evaluates to ***false***, the execution control will jump to the next ***elsif-block*** (if present) and its condition will be evaluated. This process will continue until the condition of one of the ***elsif-blocks*** evaluates to ***true*** or until there are no more ***elsif-blocks*** left while each of their conditions keep evaluating to ***false***. If none of the conditions evaluate to ***true***, the ***else-block*** (if present) will be executed.

Let us re-write the script to check whether a given number is positive, negative or zero without nesting ***if-else blocks***:

```
#if elsif else demo
#determine if an entered number is +ve, -ve or 0
#Prompt the user to enter a number
```

```
puts "\nEnter a number: \n"
num_str = gets
num_str = num_str.chomp
#Convert num_str to integer format
num = num_str.to_i()
#check if num is greater than 0
if (num > 0)
      puts "\n#{ num } is positive."
#check if num is less than 0
elsif (num < 0)
      puts "\n#{ num } is negative."
#if the number is neither positive, nor negative, then
it is 0
else
      puts "\n#{ num } is zero."
end
```

Output:

```
F:\RubyScripts>ruby pnz.rb

Enter a number:
-87

-87 is negative.

F:\RubyScripts>ruby pnz.rb

Enter a number:
0

0 is zero.

F:\RubyScripts>ruby pnz.rb

Enter a number:
17

17 is positive.

F:\RubyScripts>
```

Notes:

- An ***if-block*** can exist on its own while an ***elsif-block*** or an ***else-block*** cannot. For ***else-block*** or an ***elsif-block***, a preceding ***if-block*** is mandatory.
- Specifying a condition is required only for ***if*** and ***elsif*** statements and not for ***else*** statements.

- The ***end*** keyword marks the end of one ***if-block*** or one ***if-else block*** combination or one ***if-elsif-else*** block combination.

- One and only one block will be executed within one combination of ***if-elsif-else*** blocks. Once that happens, remaining blocks will be skipped.

- An ***if-block*** can end with the ***end*** keyword or an ***elsif*** statement or an ***else*** statement. An ***elsif-block*** can end with the ***end*** keyword or an ***else*** statement. An else block will end with the ***end*** keyword which will also mark the end of one ***if-elsif-else*** combination. Refer to the screenshot of previous two programming examples, end of blocks is marked:

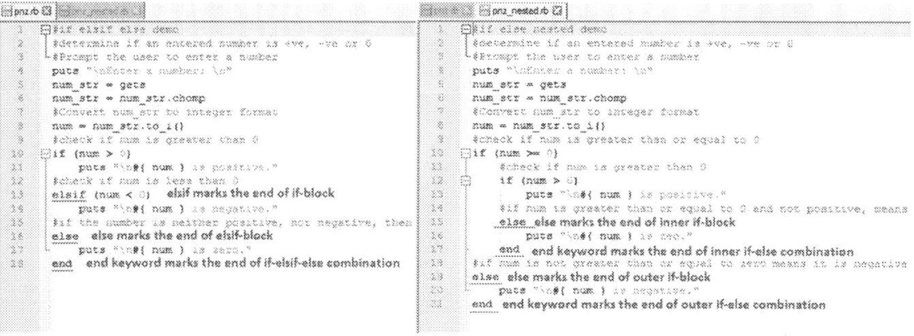

10.1.2 case-when

Ruby offers another decision making feature using the case-when construct. This is similar to switch-case construct in C/C++, C#, Java, etc. When a condition can lead to multiple outcomes, you can of course write multiple ***elsif*** statements or perhaps use nested ***if-else*** blocks but ***case-when*** construct offers a better way to deal with such a situation. General syntax:

```
case <expression>
        when <expression 1>
                #Statements to be executed when <expression>
                #Matches <expression 1>
        when <expression 2>
                #Statements to be executed when <expression>
                #Matches <expression 2>
        when <expression 3>
                #Statements to be executed when <expression>
                #Matches <expression 3>
        ...
        ...
        ...
        when <expression n>
                #Statements to be executed when <expression>
                #Matches <expression n>
        else
                #Statements to be executed when <expression>
                #DOES NOT MATCH any of the expressions
end
```

The ***case*** statement should be given an expression marked by ***<expression>*** in the above snippet. The expression can be made up of a single variable or something like a polynomial made up of multiple variables and operators. There can be various ***when*** blocks which begin with ***when*** statement. Each ***when*** statement has an expression of its own, marked by ***<expression n>*** in the above snippet. When a ***case*** statement is encountered, its expression is evaluated and a value is obtained. This value is checked against the expressions of ***when*** statements. If the value matches the expression of a when statement, that particular ***when block*** is executed and the remaining blocks are skipped. If no matching expression is found, the ***else-block*** (if present) is executed. The ***case-when*** construct ends with an ***end*** keyword. Let us write a script where we will ask the user to enter a number from 0 to 9 and display it in words. For example, if the user enters 7, "Seven" should be printed. If the user enters anything other than 0 to 9, the else block should get activated telling the user that it is an invalid option:

```
#Case When Demo
puts "\nEnter a number (0 - 9): \n"
num_str = gets
num_str = num_str.chomp
#Convert num_str to integer format
num = num_str.to_i()
case (num)
      when 0
            puts "You have entered: Zero\n"
      when 1
            puts "You have entered: One\n"
      when 2
            puts "You have entered: Two\n"
      when 3
            puts "You have entered: Three\n"
      when 4
            puts "You have entered: Four\n"
      when 5
            puts "You have entered: Five\n"
      when 6
            puts "You have entered: Six\n"
      when 7
            puts "You have entered: Seven\n"
      when 8
            puts "You have entered: Eight\n"
      when 9
            puts "You have entered: Nine\n"
      else
            puts "Invalid Option. Enter a number between
0 and 9"
end
```

Output:

```
F:\RubyScripts>ruby casewhen.rb
Enter a number (0 - 9):
5
You have entered: Five

F:\RubyScripts>ruby casewhen.rb
Enter a number (0 - 9):
0
You have entered: Zero

F:\RubyScripts>ruby casewhen.rb
Enter a number (0 - 9):
8
You have entered: Eight

F:\RubyScripts>ruby casewhen.rb
Enter a number (0 - 9):
99
Invalid Option. Enter a number between 0 and 9

F:\RubyScripts>ruby casewhen.rb
Enter a number (0 - 9):
3
You have entered: Three

F:\RubyScripts>_
```

If you want to execute one particular when block for more than one expressions, you can separate the expressions using commas as follows:

```
case <expression>:
        when <expression 1>, <expression 2>, … <expression n>
                #Statements to be executed if <expression> matches
                #<expression 1>, <expression 2>, … <expression n>
end
Example:
case val:
        when 1, 2, 3
                puts "Value is 1, 2 or 3"
end
```

The ***case-when*** construct is not just limited to matching numeric values, it can work with strings too. Let us write a script where we will as the user to enter a number from 0 to 9 in words and the script will print in numeric format. Ruby is case sensitive and hence we will have to account for user inputs such as "two", "Two" and "TWO". All of these inputs should execute the same ***when*** block:

```
#Case When Demo
puts "\nEnter a number from Zero to Nine in words: \n"
num_str = gets
num_str = num_str.chomp
case (num_str)
      when "zero", "Zero", "ZERO"
            puts "You have entered: 0\n"
      when "one", "One", "ONE"
            puts "You have entered: 1\n"
      when "two", "Two", "TWO"
            puts "You have entered: 2\n"
      when "three", "Three", "THREE"
            puts "You have entered: 3\n"
      when "four", "Four", "FOUR"
            puts "You have entered: 4\n"
      when "five", "Five", "FIVE"
            puts "You have entered: 5\n"
      when "six", "Six", "SIX"
            puts "You have entered: 6\n"
      when "seven", "Seven", "SEVEN"
            puts "You have entered: 7\n"
      when "eight", "Eight", "EIGHT"
            puts "You have entered: 8\n"
      when "nine", "Nine", "NINE"
            puts "You have entered: 9\n"
      else
            puts "Invalid Option. Enter a number between
0 and 9 in words"
end
```

<u>Output:</u>

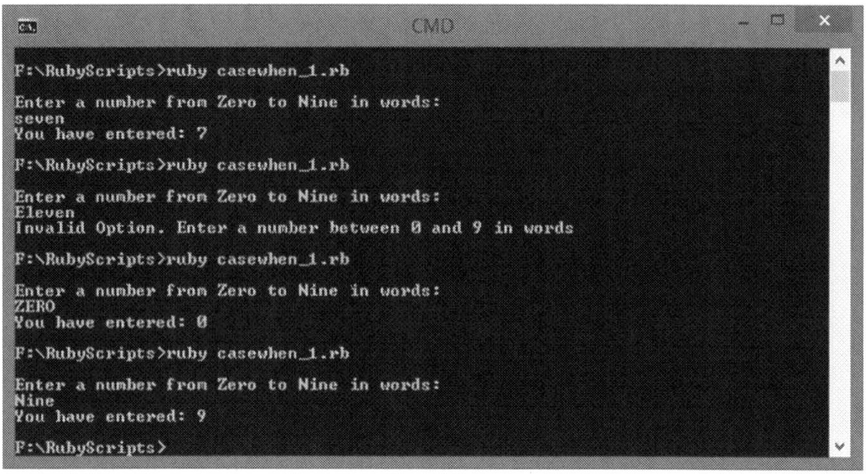

```
CMD
F:\RubyScripts>ruby casewhen_1.rb
Enter a number from Zero to Nine in words:
seven
You have entered: 7

F:\RubyScripts>ruby casewhen_1.rb
Enter a number from Zero to Nine in words:
Eleven
Invalid Option. Enter a number between 0 and 9 in words

F:\RubyScripts>ruby casewhen_1.rb
Enter a number from Zero to Nine in words:
ZERO
You have entered: 0

F:\RubyScripts>ruby casewhen_1.rb
Enter a number from Zero to Nine in words:
Nine
You have entered: 9

F:\RubyScripts>
```

10.2 Loops

Loops are programming constructs used to run a piece of code over a number of times based on whether a given condition is met or not met. Ruby offers ***while loop***, ***until loop***, ***do loop*** and ***for loop***. We will take a look at ***while, until and do*** loops in this section and ***for loop*** will be covered in the ***Arrays*** chapter.

10.2.1 while Loop

A ***while loop*** begins with a ***while*** statement and ends with the ***end*** keyword. From ***while*** statement to the ***end*** keyword marks the while loop block. General syntax:

while (<condition>) do

#Statements to be executed as long as <condition> remains true

end

Example:

```
count = 0
while (count < 10) do
        puts count
        count = count + 1
end
```

A ***while loop*** should be given a condition marked by ***<condition>*** in the above code snippet. Statements inside the ***while loop*** block will be executed as long as the given condition remains ***true***. The moment the given condition becomes ***false***, the loop stops executing and the execution control comes out of the loop block. If the condition never becomes ***false***, the loop will go on executing indefinitely and such a loop is known as an ***infinite loop***. This is how a while loop works – when a ***while*** statement is encountered, its condition is checked. If it evaluates to ***true***, the statements under the loop block are executed one by one. This is known as *one loop iteration*. When the execution control reaches the end of the loop block, the control will jump back to the ***while*** statement and the given condition will be checked again. If the condition evaluates to ***true*** again, the loop block will be executed again. This process will go on as long as the condition remains true. Normally (and absolutely not always!) a ***loop variable*** is used to keep track of the number of iterations and the condition is made up of some sought of an expression involving the loop variable. As a programmer, it is your job to initialize the loop variable before entering the loop, set a condition based on the loop variable if required and make changes to the loop variable inside the loop such as increment, decrement, etc. Let us take a look at a simple while loop example where we will print something on the screen five times:

```
#While loop demo
#Display a message 5 times
#Initialize a loop variable
count = 0
#while loop begins
while (count < 5) do
      puts "\nInside while loop!"
      #Increment loop variable
      count = count + 1
end
```

Output:

```
CMD
F:\RubyScripts>ruby whiledemo.rb
Inside while loop!
Inside while loop!
Inside while loop!
Inside while loop!
Inside while loop!
F:\RubyScripts>
```

10.2.2 until Loop

The ***until*** loop begins with an ***until*** statement and ends with the ***end*** keyword. This loop also needs a condition to work with. However, unlike while loop, the until loop goes on executing as long as the given condition is not true; i.e. the given condition after evaluation should yield ***false***. General syntax:

until <condition> do

#Statements to be executed as long as <condition> remains false.

end

Example:

until (count ==5) do

puts count

count = count + 1

end

Let us write a Ruby script to print multiples of 3 from 3 to 30 using ***until loop***:

```
#Until loop demo
#Display multiples of 3
#Initialize a loop variable
count = 1
#until loop begins
until (count == 11) do
      puts "\n#{ count * 3 }"
      #Increment loop variable
      count = count + 1
end
```

Output:

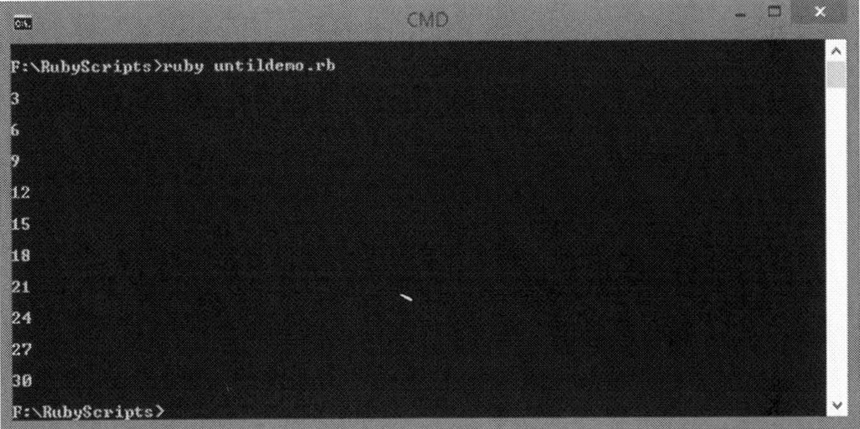

10.2.3 Loop Control Statements

Before learning how the ***do loop*** works, we need to understand what are control statements and how to use them. A loop would normally execute as long as the given condition is met or not met. If you want to alter this normal execution model of a loop, you can use control statement. Ruby offers two control statements – ***break*** and ***next***. A break statement will abruptly terminate the loop and the execution control will come out of the loop block. A ***next*** statement will skip the current iteration and move to the next one.

We will see a demo on ***break*** statement while learning the ***do loop***. Let us now see ***next*** statement in action. We will write a Ruby script to print multiples of 4 between 4 and 40 and skip if the current multiple is also a multiple of 3:

```
#next demo using While loop
#Display multiples of 4 but skip when its a multiple of 3 also
puts "\nPrinting multiples of 4 but not 3 between 4 and 40"
#Initialize a loop variable
count = 1
#while loop begins
while (count <= 10) do
      #Calculate multiple
      mul = count * 4
      #Check if mul is also a multiple of 3, if so, skip current iteration
      if ( mul % 3 == 0)
            #Increment loop variable
            count = count + 1
            #Skip iteration
            next
      end
      puts "\n#{ mul }"
      #Increment loop variable
      count = count + 1
end
```

<u>Output:</u>

```
CMD
F:\RubyScripts>ruby nextdemo.rb
Printing multiples of 4 but not 3 between 4 and 40
4
8
16
20
28
32
40
F:\RubyScripts>
```

10.2.4 do Loop

The reason why control statements are covered before ***do loop*** is because there is no way to specify a condition for ***do loop***. You have to manually check for the validity of a condition inside the loop (using ***if-else***, ***case-when***, etc.) and use the ***break*** statement to manually terminate the execution of the loop. If you do not check for the condition and terminate the loop manually, the loop will be an infinite loop on its own. The ***do loop*** begins with the ***loop do*** statement and ends with the ***end*** keyword. General Syntax:

```
loop do
        #Statements to be executed
end
```

Example:

```
loop do
        puts count
        count = count + 1
        if (count == 4)
                break
        end
end
```

Let us write a script to print numbers from 1 to 10 using do loop:

```
#do loop demo
#Display from 1 to 10
#Initialize a loop variable
count = 1
#do loop begins
loop do
      puts "\n#{ count }"
      #Check if count reached 10, if so, break
      if (count == 10)
            break
      end
      #Increment loop variable count
      count = count + 1
end
```

<u>Output:</u>

```
F:\RubyScripts>ruby doloop.rb
1
2
3
4
5
6
7
8
9
10
F:\RubyScripts>_
```

11. Methods

A ***method*** is a piece of code when called to activate performs a task or a set of tasks. ***Methods*** are also known as ***functions, routines or sub-routines***. So far, we have used several methods such as ***puts*** (to print on the console), ***gets*** (prompt to receive input from the user), ***to_i*** (convert string to integer), etc. These were built-in methods. In this chapter, we will learn to write our own methods and use them. There are two important concepts when learning methods – ***method definition*** and ***method call.***

11.1 Defining a method/function

A method definition begins with a ***def*** keyword and ends with the ***end*** keyword. General Syntax:

```
def <method_name> (<parameters>)
        #Statements to be executed when this method is called
end
Example:
def myMethod( )
        print "This is a method demo!"
end
```

A function can optionally accept a *list of parameters* marked by ***<parameters>*** in the above code snippet. Parameters in the function definition are variables used to receive data and are also called ***arguments***. A method can accept multiple parameters by separating them using commas. Let us define a method to print a message on the console, try to execute the script and see what happens:

```
#Simple method demo
#Method definition
def simpleMethod()
      puts "\nInside simpleMethod. Hello World Again!"
end
```

Output:

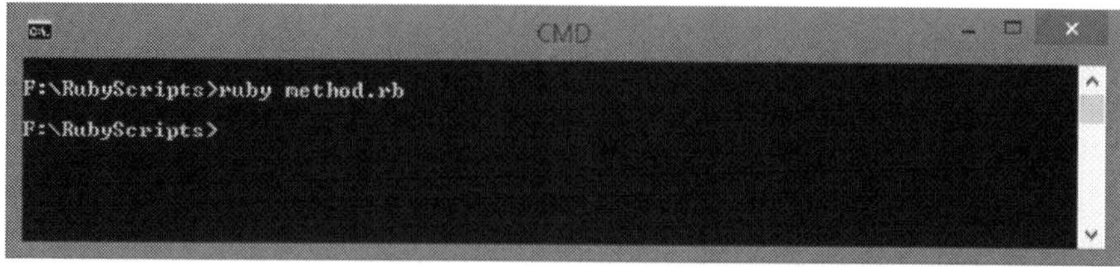

As you can see from the code and the output, although we are trying to print a message inside ***simpleMethod*** function, nothing is printed on the console. This is because the method is there but it is not called.

Note: It is best to put all the function definitions in the beginning of the script.

11.2 Calling a method/function

It is evident from the previous example that a function cannot work on its own. To activate a method block, a call must be made to that method. General syntax:

> *<function name> <parameters>*
>
> *Example:*
>
> *myMethod*

Let us make changes to the previous code and add a function call to ***simpleMethod***:

```
#Simple method demo
#Method definition
def simpleMethod()
      puts "\nInside simpleMethod. Hello World Again!"
end
#Execution begins here
puts "\nExecution begins, calling simpleMethod"
#Call simpleMethod
simpleMethod
puts "\nOutside simpleMethod. Script coming to an end."
```

Output:

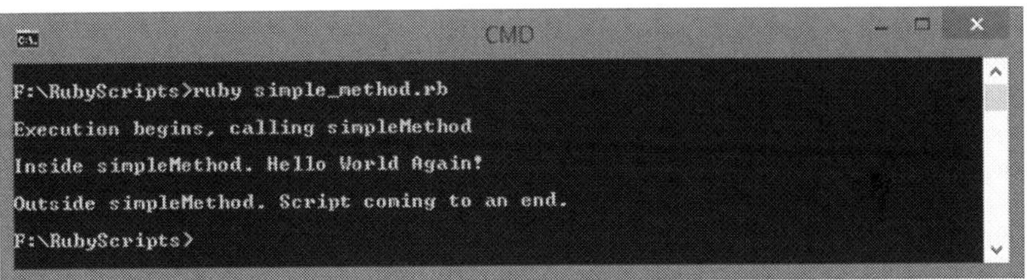

To avoid confusion, the screenshot of the above code has been marked to show the line where script execution begins:

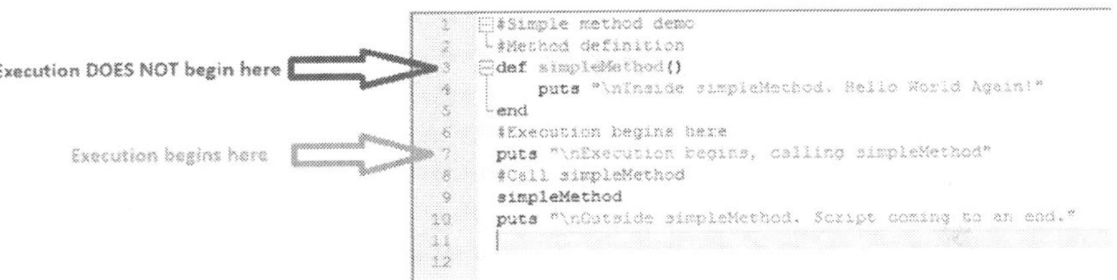

11.3 Passing parameters to a method/function

We have used the ***puts*** function so many times now. After the ***puts*** statement, we specify a string which then gets printed. What happens over there is, we pass a string as a parameter to the ***puts*** method. Let us now learn how to write our own methods which accept parameters. General syntax:

def <method name> (<parameter 1>, <parameter 2>, … <parameter n>)

#Statements…

end

Example:

def triple (num)

*t = num * 3*

puts t

end

When calling a function that accepts parameters, the same number of parameters should be passed as mentioned in the function definition (there are some exceptions to this rule). General syntax:

<method name> <parameter 1>, <parameter 2>, …, <parameter n>

Example:

triple 6

Let us write a function that accepts 3 parameters and displays them inside the function using ***puts***:

```
#Pass arguments to method
#Method definition
def demoMethod(msg1, msg2, msg3)
      puts "\nInside demoMethod\n"
      puts "\nMessage 1: #{ msg1 } \nMessage 2: #{ msg2
} \nMessage 3: #{ msg3 }"
end
#Execution begins here
puts "\nExecution begins, calling demoMethod and passing
some string values as arguments"
#Call demoMethod
demoMethod "This is", "another method demo", "these
messages are passed arguments"
puts "\nOutside demoMethod. Script coming to an end."
```

Output:

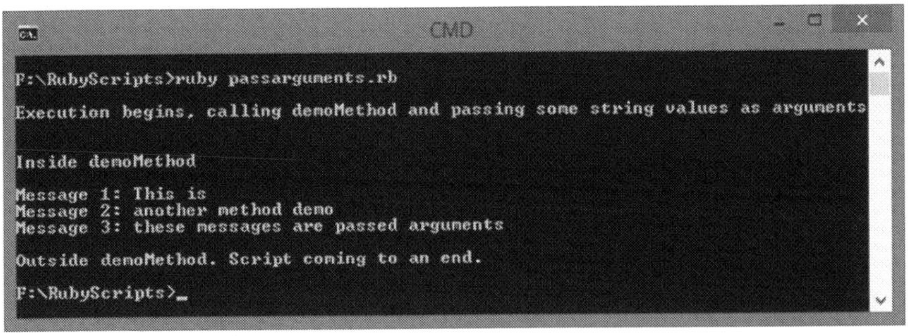

```
CMD
F:\RubyScripts>ruby passarguments.rb
Execution begins, calling demoMethod and passing some string values as arguments

Inside demoMethod
Message 1: This is
Message 2: another method demo
Message 3: these messages are passed arguments

Outside demoMethod. Script coming to an end.
F:\RubyScripts>_
```

11.4 Return values

A function can return values back to the statement which calls the function using the return keyword. A variable must be used to receive the returned value otherwise the value may get lost. General syntax:

def <method name> (<parameters>)
#Statements
return <variable/constant/expression>
end

Example:

def quadruple (x)
*quad = 4 * x*
return quad
end

A variable can be used to receive the returned value as follows:

<variable> = <method name>(<parameters>)

Example:

q = quadruple (8)

Note: You can return as many values as you want by separating them with commas. When two or more values are returned, they are received as an ***array***. This concept is covered in the ***Arrays*** chapter. In this section we will focus on returning single value only.

Let us write a script with 5 functions to perform arithmetic operations and return the result:

```
#Pass arguments and return values
#Method definitions
#Method to find sum
def getSum (x, y)
      sum = x + y
      return sum
end
#Method to find difference
def getDiff (x, y)
      diff = x - y
      return diff
end
#Method to find product
def getProd (x, y)
      prod = x * y
      return prod
end
#Method to find quotient
def getQuo (x, y)
      q = x / y
      return q
end
#Method to find exp
def getExp (x, y)
      exp = x ** y
      return exp
end
#Execution begins here
#Define two variables
a = 4.67
b = 8.24
puts "\na = #{ a } b = #{ b }\n"
#Call methods one by one
s = getSum a, b
d = getDiff a, b
p = getProd a, b
q = getQuo a, b
ex = getExp a, b
#Print everything
puts "\na + b = #{ s } \na - b = #{ d } \na * b = #{ p
} \na / b = #{ q } \na ** b = #{ ex }"
```

Output:

```
CMD
F:\RubyScripts>ruby method_return.rb
a = 4.67 b = 8.24
a + b = 12.91
a - b = -3.5700000000000003
a * b = 38.4808
a / b = 0.5667475728155340
a ** b = 327469.6803375807
F:\RubyScripts>
```

11.5 Default Parameters

Default values can be set to parameters. In such cases, the default parameters need not be passed during function call. When default parameters are not passed, the default values will be considered and when values for default parameters are passed, the default values will be overridden and the passed values will be considered. Default parameters can be set from the rightmost parameter in a sequential manner. General syntax:

def <method name> (<parameter> = <default value>)

#Statements

#Optional return statement

end

Example:

def sampleMethod (param1, param2, param3 = 50)

puts param1, param2, param3

end

Let us demonstrate the working of default parameters. We will write a method called ***getArea*** which can calculate the area of a rectangle as well as a circle. The way this function works is as follows – The area of a rectangle is given by *A = length x width* and the area of a circle is given by $A = \pi r^2$ which can be also written as $A = \pi\ x\ r\ x\ r$. In the ***getArea*** method, if we could receive 3 parameters, multiply them to determine area and make sure that the third parameter is ***pi (3.14)*** for circle and ***1*** for rectangle, we have a function that can calculate the area of two geometric figures:

```
#Default parameters demo
#Defining a function that can calculate the area of a cirle as well as a rectangle
def getArea (x, y, pi = 1)
      area = x * y * pi
      return area
end
#Area of a rectangle with length 8 and width 5
#Just pass two arguments, leng and width
length = 8
width = 5
area_rect = getArea length, width
#Area of a circle with radius 7
#Just pass three arguments arguments, radius twice and pi as 3.14
radius = 7
pi = 3.14
area_circle = getArea radius, radius, pi
puts "\nArea of a rectangle:\n"
puts "\nLength: #{ length } Width: #{ width } Area: #{ area_rect }"
puts "\nArea of a circle:\n"
puts "\nLength: #{ radius } Area: #{ area_circle }"
```

Output:

```
F:\RubyScripts>ruby defaultargs.rb
Area of a rectangle:
Length: 8 Width: 5 Area: 40
Area of a circle:
Length: 7 Area: 153.86
F:\RubyScripts>
```

11.6 Local v/s Global variables

Variables declared within a method block are only accessible inside that method only. Such variables are known as local variables because they are local to that method. If you try to access a variable declared inside a method from another method, there is going to be an error. Global variables are declared outside all functions with a ***dollar sign ($)*** prefixed to the variable name. These kind of variables can be accessed from all methods and their value will be common. Changes made to a global variable in one method can be seen in another method.

12. Arrays

An ***array*** is a data structure used to store *a collection of items.* An item in an array could be data of any data type. Mixed data types are also allowed. Individual elements of an array can be accessed with the help of their ***index***. Array index *begins at 0* and goes up to *one less than the size of the array*. For example, if an array has 20 elements, the first element will be present at index 0 and the last element will be present at index 19.

12.1 Array Creation and Basics

An array can be created in a number of ways. We will take a look at a few methods. An empty array can be created using ***Array.new*** function. General syntax:

> *<array variable> = Array.new (<array size>)*
> *Example:*
> *Names = Array.new (10)*

The ***Array.new*** function simply reserves the said amount of memory locations for an array. There are no elements yet. If you want to fill data into an array at the time of creation, you can use the following syntax:

> *<array variable> = Array [<value 1>, … <value n>]*
> *Example:*
> *Num = Array [1, 7, -5, 4.7]*

In the above example, ***1*** is present at ***index 0***, ***7*** is present at ***index 1***, ***-5*** is present at ***index 2*** and ***4.7*** is present at ***index 3***. This is how this array would look inside the memory:

Array - Num

Values -->	1	7	-5	4.7
Index -->	0	1	2	3

Individual elements can be fetched or set with the help of the access operator and the index as follows:

```
#Retrieve elements:
<variable> = <array variable>[index]
Example:
Name = data[1]
#Set element values
<array variable>[index] = <variable/constant/expression>
Example:
arr[0] = 9
arr[1] = 2
arr[3] = 5
```

If an array is created using ***Array.new*** method, you can always add elements later. In an existing array, you can even add an element at an index greater than size of the array. In such a case, the array size will automatically increase and the new element will be placed at the specified index. *If the new index is not exactly one more than previous last index*, this method will still work – the array size will be appropriately augmented, new intermediate locations will be created between the previous last index and the new index. Those locations will have the value ***nil*** which is equivalent to ***null***. For example, if an array has 3 elements and you try to add a 4th element at index 3, this situation is straight forward. But if you try to add a 4th element at say index 7, the array size will grow to

8, your new element will be placed at index 7 as desired and values at index 4 to index 6 will be set to ***nil***.

Array size can be determined with the help of ***<array variable>.length*** or ***<array variable>.size*** methods. Let us put these concepts to use and write a Ruby script where we will create two arrays – one will be initialized at the time of creation and the other will be assigned values later. The contents of the arrays will be displayed index by index:

```
#Array Demo
sample_array = Array.new(5)
num_array = Array [3, 6, -7, 1.45, -4, 9, 1]
#Print array contents and size
puts "\nsample_array size: #{ sample_array.length }
\n\nsample_array contents:\n\n #{ sample_array }"
puts "\nnum_array size: #{ num_array.length }
\n\nnum_array contents:\n\n #{ num_array }"
#Add five elements to sample_array
sample_array[0] = "Hello"
sample_array[1] = "World"
sample_array[2] = 5.8
sample_array[3] = -33
sample_array[4] = "USA"
#Add one extra element at index 5, array size will
automatically increase by 1
sample_array[5] = "GM"
#Print contents of both arrays index by index
puts "\nsample_array size: #{ sample_array.length }
\n\nsample_array contents:\n\n #{ sample_array }"
puts "\nIndex 0 => sample_array[0]: #{ sample_array[0]
}"
puts "\nIndex 1 => sample_array[1]: #{ sample_array[1]
}"
puts "\nIndex 2 => sample_array[2]: #{ sample_array[2]
}"
puts "\nIndex 3 => sample_array[3]: #{ sample_array[3]
}"
puts "\nIndex 4 => sample_array[4]: #{ sample_array[4]
}"
puts "\nIndex 5 => sample_array[5]: #{ sample_array[5]
}"
```

```
puts "\nnum_array size: #{ num_array.length } \n\nnum_array contents:\n\n #{ num_array }"
puts "\nIndex 0 => num_array[0]: #{ num_array[0] }"
puts "\nIndex 1 => num_array[1]: #{ num_array[1] }"
puts "\nIndex 2 => num_array[2]: #{ num_array[2] }"
puts "\nIndex 3 => num_array[3]: #{ num_array[3] }"
puts "\nIndex 4 => num_array[4]: #{ num_array[4] }"
```

Output:

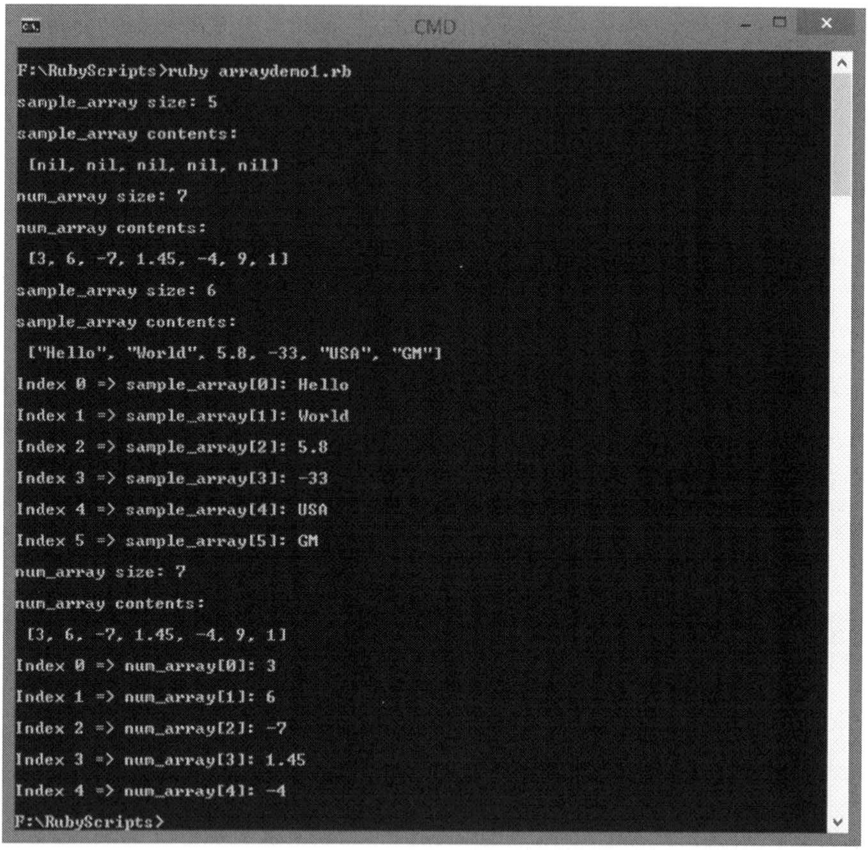

```
CMD
F:\RubyScripts>ruby arraydemo1.rb
sample_array size: 5
sample_array contents:
 [nil, nil, nil, nil, nil]
num_array size: 7
num_array contents:
 [3, 6, -7, 1.45, -4, 9, 1]
sample_array size: 6
sample_array contents:
 ["Hello", "World", 5.8, -33, "USA", "GM"]
Index 0 => sample_array[0]: Hello
Index 1 => sample_array[1]: World
Index 2 => sample_array[2]: 5.8
Index 3 => sample_array[3]: -33
Index 4 => sample_array[4]: USA
Index 5 => sample_array[5]: GM
num_array size: 7
num_array contents:
 [3, 6, -7, 1.45, -4, 9, 1]
Index 0 => num_array[0]: 3
Index 1 => num_array[1]: 6
Index 2 => num_array[2]: -7
Index 3 => num_array[3]: 1.45
Index 4 => num_array[4]: -4
F:\RubyScripts>
```

Array indexes are assigned sequentially. Instead of accounting for each and every index manually, we can use loops to go through the index from 0 to size – 1 or whatever is desired. Here is an example:

```
#Array and loops
#Initialize an array
names = Array["Booker", "Carla", "Shane", "Phil",
"Willie"]
puts "\nnames array size: #{ names.length } \n\nnames
array contents:\n"
#Initialize a loop variable
count = 0
#while loop begins
#Loop from 0 to names.length
while (count < names.length) do
      #Print array elements
      puts "\nIndex: #{ count } names[#{ count }]: #{
names[count] }"
      #Increment loop variable
      count = count + 1
end
```

Output:

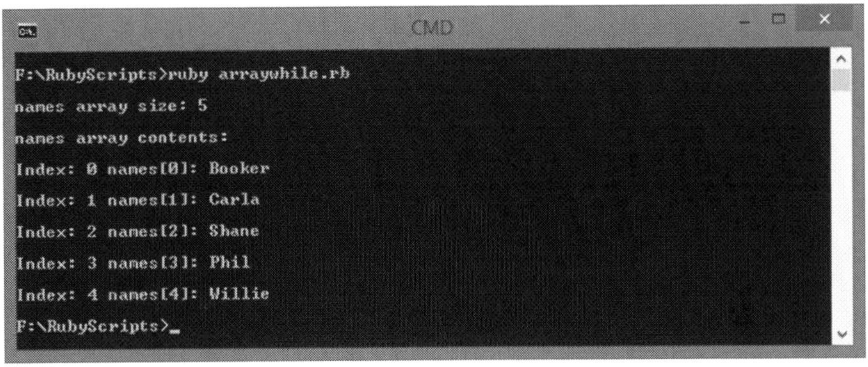

```
CMD
F:\RubyScripts>ruby arraywhile.rb
names array size: 5
names array contents:
Index: 0 names[0]: Booker
Index: 1 names[1]: Carla
Index: 2 names[2]: Shane
Index: 3 names[3]: Phil
Index: 4 names[4]: Willie
F:\RubyScripts>_
```

Notice how size of the code becomes significantly less when loops are used with arrays.

12.2 Reading user input into Arrays

Input can be read from the user using the ***gets*** function, processed and stored into the individual locations of an array manually or you can use loops to do the same. Bear in mind that when using loops, the ***gets*** function needs to be inside the loop. Here is an example where a while loop runs 5 times to read 5 numbers as input from the user. As an added step, we calculate the sum and the average of the entered numbers.

```
#Array as input
#Declare an empty array of 5 elements
num_array = Array.new(5)
#Initialize a loop variable
index = 0
#Loop for 5 times, read 5 numbers as inputs
while (index < num_array.length) do
      #Read array elements
      #Prompt the user to enter a number
      puts "\nEnter number at index #{ index }: \n"
      num_str = gets
      num_str = num_str.chomp
      #Convert num_str to float format
      num = num_str.to_f()
      #Add num to num_array at current index
      num_array[index] = num
      #Increment loop variable
      index = index + 1
end
#Print array contents
#Initialize a loop variable again
index = 0
#Initialize sum variable
sum = 0
#while loop begins
#Loop from 0 to num_array.length
while (index < num_array.length) do
      #Print array elements
      puts "\nIndex: #{ index } num_array[#{ index }]:
#{ num_array[index] }"
      #Calculate sum
      sum += num_array[index]
      #Increment loop variable
      index = index + 1
end
#Display sum and average
puts "\n\nSum = #{ sum } \tAverage = #{ sum/5.0 }\n"
```

Output:

```
F:\RubyScripts>ruby arrayinput.rb
Enter number at index 0:
-56.3
Enter number at index 1:
104.87
Enter number at index 2:
-23.45
Enter number at index 3:
12.75
Enter number at index 4:
43.87
Index: 0 num_array[0]: -56.3
Index: 1 num_array[1]: 104.87
Index: 2 num_array[2]: -23.45
Index: 3 num_array[3]: 12.75
Index: 4 num_array[4]: 43.87

Sum = 81.74000000000001          Average = 16.348000000000003
F:\RubyScripts>_
```

12.3 for Loop and Arrays

This section is a sort of an augmentation of the ***Loops*** chapter. ***for loop*** was excluded from that chapter because it works only with ranges or iterative data types such as arrays. General Syntax:

for <element variable> in <range/array>

#Statements

end

Example:

for x in numbers

puts x

end

A for loop needs two things to work – element variable marked by ***<element variable>*** in the code snippet and a range or an array marked by ***<range/array>***. During the first iteration, the element at index 0 (first element) will be fetched into the element variable automatically. During the next iteration, the next element will be fetched. This process will go on until the end of array is reached. Let us modify the previous programming example. We will read five elements using ***while loop*** and print those elements using ***for loop***:

```
#Array as input
#Output using for loop
#Declare an empty array of 5 elements
num_array = Array.new(5)
#Initialize a loop variable
index = 0
#Loop for 5 times, read 5 numbers as inputs
while (index < num_array.length) do
      #Read array elements
      #Prompt the user to enter a number
      puts "\nEnter number at index #{ index }: \n"
      num_str = gets
      num_str = num_str.chomp
      #Convert num_str to float format
      num = num_str.to_f()
      #Add num to num_array at current index
      num_array[index] = num
      #Increment loop variable
      index = index + 1
end
puts "\nnum_array contents printed using for loop:\n\n"
for element in num_array
      puts "#{ element }"
end
```

Output:

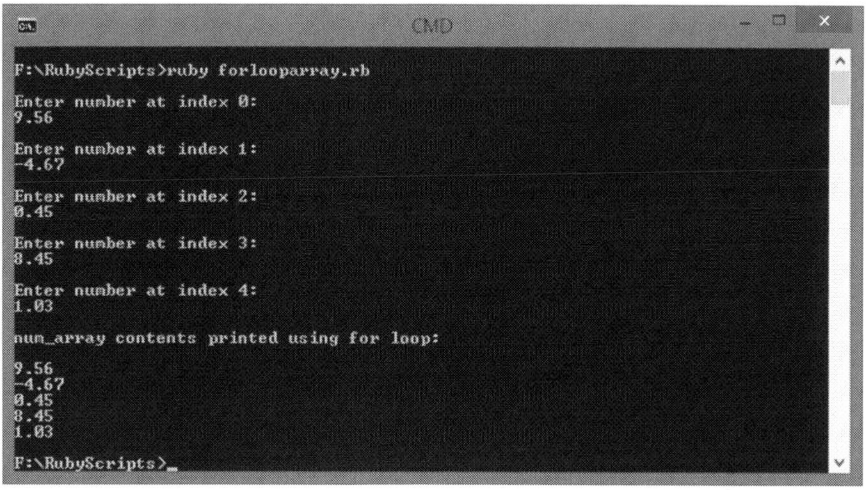

```
F:\RubyScripts>ruby forlooparray.rb
Enter number at index 0:
9.56
Enter number at index 1:
-4.67
Enter number at index 2:
0.45
Enter number at index 3:
8.45
Enter number at index 4:
1.03
num_array contents printed using for loop:
9.56
-4.67
0.45
8.45
1.03
F:\RubyScripts>_
```

12.4 Return multiple values from a method

In the methods chapter, under ***Section 10.4***, we saw how a method can return a single value back to the calling statement. In this section, we will understand how to return two or more values and how to receive them.

Multiple values can be returned by separating values using commas. These values are implicitly packaged into an array and sent. In the calling statement, there should be a variable to receive these values. The receiving variable become an array. The first returned value is placed at index 0, the second one at index 1, the third one at index 2 and so on. Return syntax:

return <value 1>, <value 2>, …., <value n>

Example:

return a, b, c, d

Let us write a script to accept two numbers from the user as input, pass these numbers as parameters to a method which computes sum, difference, product and quotient; returns all these values in a single statement:

```
#Multiple Return
def calc(x, y)
      #Perform arithmetic operations
      sum = x + y
      diff = x - y
      prod = x * y
      quo = x / y
      #Return everything
      return sum, diff, prod, quo
end
#Prompt the user to enter a number
puts "Enter a number: "
num1_str = gets
num1_str = num1_str.chomp
#Prompt the user to enter another number
puts "Enter another number: "
num2_str = gets
num2_str = num2_str.chomp
#Convert num1_str and num2_str to float formats
num1 = num1_str.to_f()
num2 = num2_str.to_f()
#Call calc function
data = calc(num1, num2)
#Print everything
puts "\nSum: #{ data[0] } \nDifference: #{ data[1] }
\nProduct: #{ data[2] } \nQuotient: #{ data[3] }"
#For Reference print data details
puts "\nDetails of array which was formed when multiple
values were returned."
puts "\ndata array size: #{ data.length } \n\ndata array
contents:\n\n #{ data }"
```

Output:

```
F:\RubyScripts>ruby multireturn.rb
Enter a number:
19
Enter another number:
7

Sum: 26.0
Difference: 12.0
Product: 133.0
Quotient: 2.7142857142857144

Details of array which was formed when multiple values were returned.

data array size: 4

data array contents:

 [26.0, 12.0, 133.0, 2.7142857142857144]

F:\RubyScripts>
```

13. Hashes

Hashes are data structures used to store a collection of items in ***key-value*** pairs. You can use the concept of arrays in order to understand hashes well. Arrays store a collection of items at indexes which run from 0 to one less than the size of the array. In hashes, a key is an equivalent of an index. Consider a hash key as a meaningful index. For example, if you want to store details of a person then keys could be name, address, age, etc. while values could be the actual details of that person at appropriate keys. Key-value pairs can be of any data type.

13.1 Creating Hashes

An empty hash can be created using ***Hash.new*** function as follows:

<hash variable> = Hash.new

#OR

<hash variable> = Hash.new()

Example:

myhash = Hash.new

This method will create an empty hash. There will be no data in it. In order to add data, you can add key-value pairs using the following syntax:

<hash variable> = {[key 1] => [value 1], [key 2] => [value 2], … [key n] => [value n]}

Example:

#Create an empty hash

Person = Hash.new

#Add details using key-value pairs

Person = {'name' = "Sam", 'age' = 19, 'country' = "Netherlands"}

Alternatively, you can directly add key-value pairs to a hash variable without creating an empty hash first. For this we use the ***Hash*** class as follows:

<hash variable> = Hash[[key 1] => [value 1], [key 2] => [value 2], … [key n] => [value n]]

Example:

Person = Hash ['name' = "Sam", 'age' = 19, 'country' = "Netherlands"]

In the above example, there is a hash variable called ***Person*** having 3 key-value pairs. Here are the details:

Hash - Person

key	*value*
'name'	*'Sam'*
'age'	*19*
'country'	*'Netherlands'*

Here is how this hash will look in the memory:

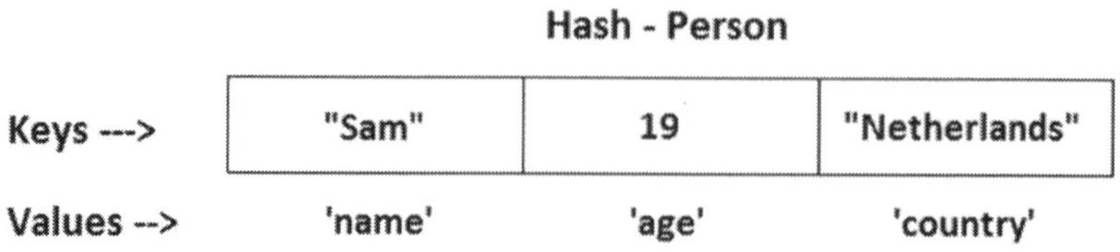

Hash - Person

Keys --->	**"Sam"**	**19**	**"Netherlands"**
Values -->	**'name'**	**'age'**	**'country'**

13.2 Hash Operations

Once you have a hash with key-value pairs, you can print the entire hash using the ***puts*** functions as follows:

> *puts "# { <hash variable> }"*
>
> *Example:*
>
> *puts "#{ myhash }"*

Individual elements of a hash can be accessed using keys as follows:

> *<hash variable>[<key>]*
>
> *Example:*
>
> *puts "#{ myhash["name"] }"*

Let us write a program to create two hashes and display their contents:

```
#Hash Demo
#Create a new hash
phone1 = Hash["make" => "OnePlus", "model" => "7t Pro",
"chipset" => "Snapdragon 855", "ram" => "8 GB", "storage"
=> "128 GB"]
#Create another Hash
phone2 = Hash.new
phone2  =  {"make"  =>  "Samsung",  "model"  =>  "S20+",
"chipset" => "Exynos 990", "ram" => "12 GB", "storage"
=> "256 GB"}
#Print both hashes
puts "\n\nHash phone1 - Complete Dump\n\n #{ phone1 }
\n\nHash phone2 - Complete Dump\n\n #{ phone2 }"
#Print both hashes in key value pairs
puts "\n\nHash phone1\n\nkey\t\tvalue\n"
puts "\nmake\t\t#{ phone1["make"] }"
puts "model\t\t#{ phone1["model"] }"
puts "chipset\t\t#{ phone1["chipset"] }"
puts "ram\t\t#{ phone1["ram"] }"
puts "storage\t\t#{ phone1["storage"] }"
puts "\n\nHash phone2\n\nkey\t\tvalue\n"
puts "\nmake\t\t#{ phone2["make"] }"
```

```
puts "model\t\t#{ phone2["model"] }"
puts "chipset\t\t#{ phone2["chipset"] }"
puts "ram\t\t#{ phone2["ram"] }"
puts "storage\t\t#{ phone2["storage"] }"
```

Output:

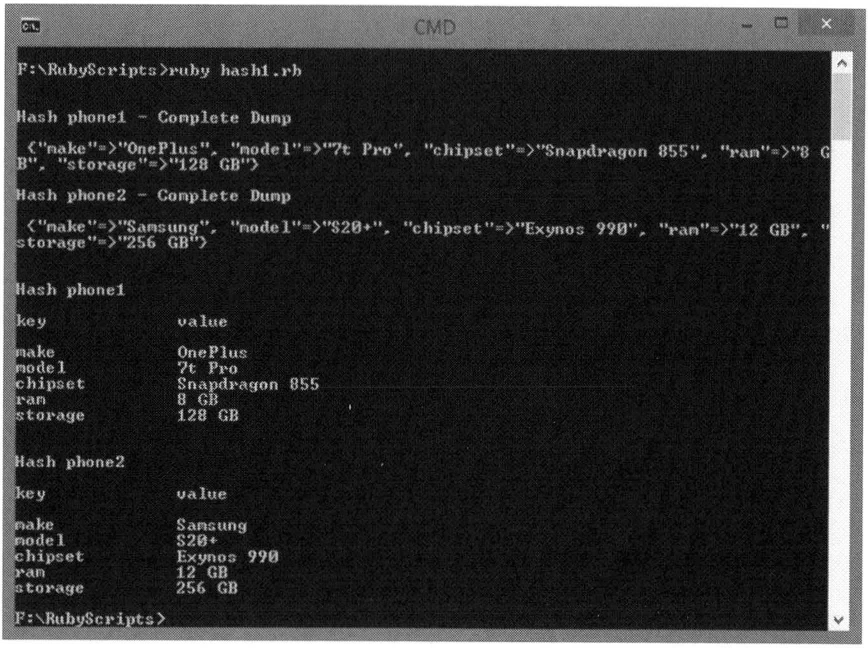

```
CMD
F:\RubyScripts>ruby hash1.rb

Hash phone1 - Complete Dump

 {"make"=>"OnePlus", "model"=>"7t Pro", "chipset"=>"Snapdragon 855", "ram"=>"8 G
B", "storage"=>"128 GB"}

Hash phone2 - Complete Dump

 {"make"=>"Samsung", "model"=>"S20+", "chipset"=>"Exynos 990", "ram"=>"12 GB", "
storage"=>"256 GB"}


Hash phone1

key             value

make            OnePlus
model           7t Pro
chipset         Snapdragon 855
ram             8 GB
storage         128 GB


Hash phone2

key             value

make            Samsung
model           S20+
chipset         Exynos 990
ram             12 GB
storage         256 GB

F:\RubyScripts>
```

13.2.1 Hash Length

The length of a hash can be determined using the ***length( )*** function. General syntax:

<length variable> = <hash variable>.length( )

Example:

Len = myhash.length( )

13.2.2 Add or update key-value pairs

A new key-value pair can be added to an existing hash using the following syntax:

<hash variable>[<key>] = <value>

Example:

Person["last_name"] = "Jordan"

If the key already exists, the existing value will be updated.

13.2.3 Delete a key-value pair

A key-value pair can be deleted using the ***delete( )*** function. General Syntax:

<hash variable>.delete(<key>)

Example:

Person.delete("age")

Let us write a Ruby script to demonstrate these hash operations:

```
#Hash operations demo
#Create a new hash
laptop = Hash["make" => "Dell", "model" => "XPS 15",
"cpu" => "Intel Core i7", "ram" => "8 GB", "storage" =>
"1 TB SSD", "display" => 15]
#Fetch length
len = laptop.length()
#Print everything
puts "\n\nHash laptop\n\nLength: #{ len }
\n\nkey\t\tvalue\n"
puts "\nmake\t\t#{ laptop["make"] }"
puts "model\t\t#{ laptop["model"] }"
puts "cpu\t\t#{ laptop["cpu"] }"
puts "ram\t\t#{ laptop["ram"] }"
puts "storage\t\t#{ laptop["storage"] }"
puts "display\t\t#{ laptop["display"] }"
#Update Hash
laptop["ram"] = "16 GB"
laptop["gpu"] = "nVidia RTX 2080"
laptop["battery"] = "86 Whr"
#Fetch length
len = laptop.length()
puts "\n\nHash laptop [After Updating]\n\nLength: #{ len
} \n\nkey\t\tvalue\n"
puts "\nmake\t\t#{ laptop["make"] }"
puts "model\t\t#{ laptop["model"] }"
```

```
puts "cpu\t\t#{ laptop["cpu"] }"
puts "ram\t\t#{ laptop["ram"] }"
puts "storage\t\t#{ laptop["storage"] }"
puts "display\t\t#{ laptop["display"] }"
puts "gpu\t\t#{ laptop["gpu"] }"
puts "battery\t\t#{ laptop["battery"] }"
#Delete key display
laptop.delete("display")
#Fetch length
len = laptop.length()
#Display updated hash all together
puts "\n\nHash laptop - Complete Dump\n\nLength: #{ len
}\n\n #{ laptop }\n"
```

<u>Output:</u>

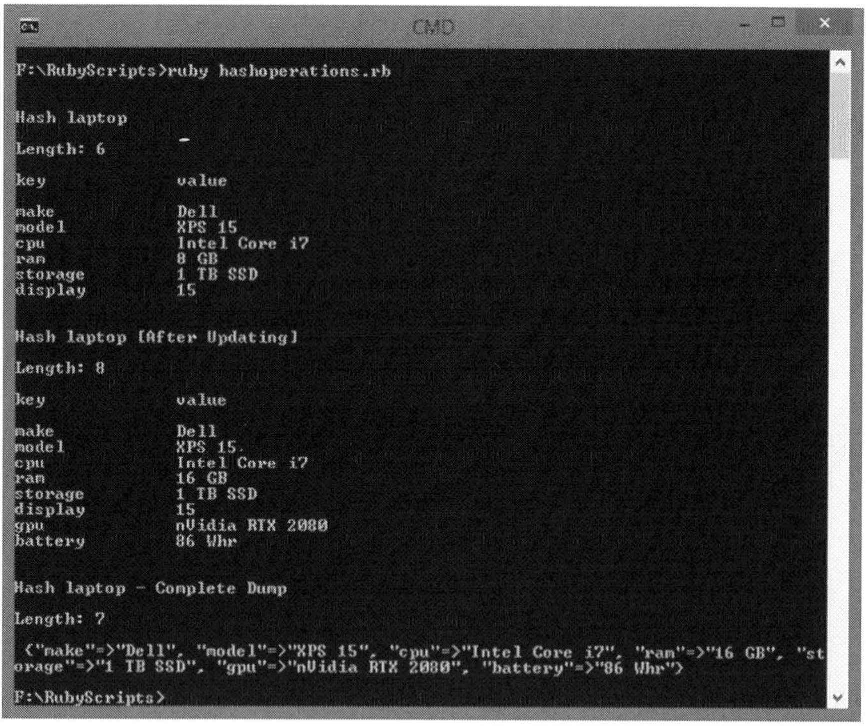

```
CMD
F:\RubyScripts>ruby hashoperations.rb

Hash laptop

Length: 6

key             value

make            Dell
model           XPS 15
cpu             Intel Core i7
ram             8 GB
storage         1 TB SSD
display         15

Hash laptop [After Updating]

Length: 8

key             value

make            Dell
model           XPS 15
cpu             Intel Core i7
ram             16 GB
storage         1 TB SSD
display         15
gpu             nVidia RTX 2080
battery         86 Whr

Hash laptop - Complete Dump

Length: 7

 {"make"=>"Dell", "model"=>"XPS 15", "cpu"=>"Intel Core i7", "ram"=>"16 GB", "st
orage"=>"1 TB SSD", "gpu"=>"nVidia RTX 2080", "battery"=>"86 Whr"}

F:\RubyScripts>
```

13.3 Fetch Keys and Values

Keys of a hash can be fetched into an array using the keys function and values can be fetched using the values function. General syntax:

<keys array variable> = <hash variable>.keys( )

<values array variable> = <hash variable>.values( )

Example:

K = myhash.keys( )

V = myhash.values( )

Here is a Ruby script that demonstrates how to fetch keys and values from a hash variable and also demonstrates how to use loops and fetched keys/values arrays to iterate through a hash variable:

```
#Hash operations continued
#Create a hash
country_capital = Hash.new()
country_capital = { "Canada" => "Ottawa", "Ireland" =>
"Dublin", "Zimbabwe" => "Harare", "Uzbekistan" =>
"Tashkent", "Singapore" => "Singapore", "Latvia" =>
"Riga" }
#Print hash
puts "\n\nHash country_capital - Length: #{
country_capital.length() } - Complete Dump\n\n #{
country_capital }"

#Fetch keys and values into arrays
countries = country_capital.keys()
capitals = country_capital.values()
#Print country and capital
puts "\n\nCountries array - Length: #{
countries.length() }\n\n"
for country in countries
      puts country
end
puts "\n\nCapitals array - Length: #{ capitals.length()
}\n\n"
for capital in capitals
      puts capital
end
#Print key value pair using while loop
```

```
puts "\n\nPrinting key-value pairs using while loop.\n\n"
count = 0
while (count < country_capital.length())
      puts "Key at index #{ count } - #{ countries[count] } \tValue at key #{ countries[count] } - #{ country_capital[countries[count]] } "
      count = count + 1
end
```

Output:

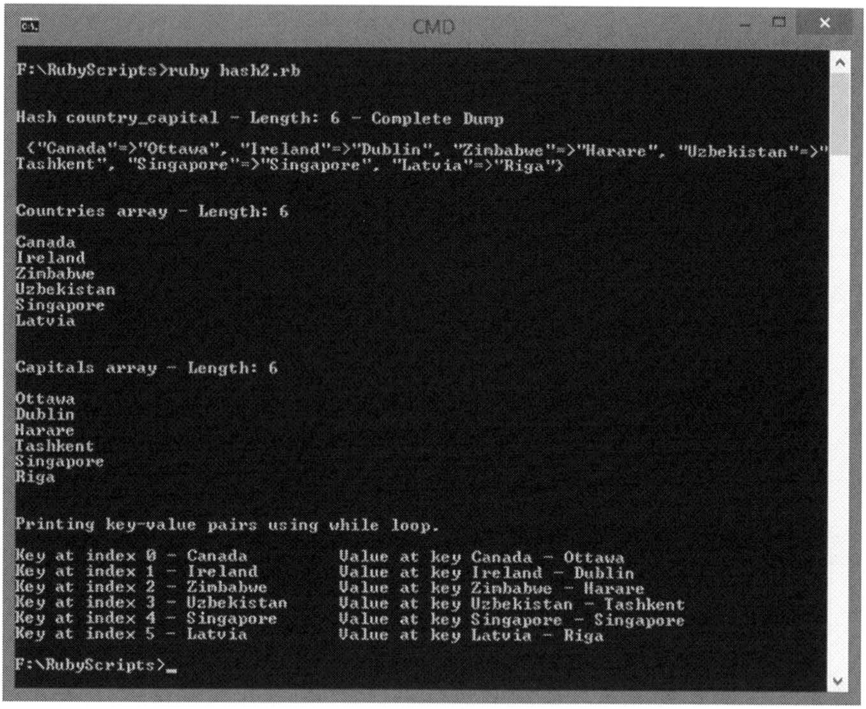

```
CMD
F:\RubyScripts>ruby hash2.rb

Hash country_capital - Length: 6 - Complete Dump

 {"Canada"=>"Ottawa", "Ireland"=>"Dublin", "Zimbabwe"=>"Harare", "Uzbekistan"=>"
Tashkent", "Singapore"=>"Singapore", "Latvia"=>"Riga"}

Countries array - Length: 6

Canada
Ireland
Zimbabwe
Uzbekistan
Singapore
Latvia

Capitals array - Length: 6

Ottawa
Dublin
Harare
Tashkent
Singapore
Riga


Printing key-value pairs using while loop.

Key at index 0 - Canada         Value at key Canada - Ottawa
Key at index 1 - Ireland        Value at key Ireland - Dublin
Key at index 2 - Zimbabwe       Value at key Zimbabwe - Harare
Key at index 3 - Uzbekistan     Value at key Uzbekistan - Tashkent
Key at index 4 - Singapore      Value at key Singapore - Singapore
Key at index 5 - Latvia         Value at key Latvia - Riga

F:\RubyScripts>_
```

13.4 Form hashes using user-input

You can read keys and values from the user and create dynamic hashes. Here is a script that reads 5 key-value pairs, forms a hash with it and then displays the contents:

```
#Hash as input
#Create an empty hash
```

```
user_hash = Hash.new
#Run while loop for 5 times, take 5 inputs
count = 0
while (count < 5)
      #Read key
      #Prompt the user key
      puts "\nEnter a key at index #{ count }: \n"
      key = gets
      key = key.chomp
      #Read value
      #Prompt the user value
      puts "\nEnter the value at key #{ key }: \n"
      value = gets
      value = value.chomp
      #Add key-value pair to the hash
      user_hash[key] = value
      count = count + 1
end
#Print hash
puts "\n\nHash user_hash - Length: #{ user_hash.length()
} - Complete Dump\n\n #{ user_hash }"
#Fetch keys and values into arrays
user_hash_keys = user_hash.keys()
user_hash_values = user_hash.values()
#Print user_hash_keys user_hash_values
puts   "\n\nuser_hash_keys   array   -   Length:   #{
user_hash_keys.length() }\n\n"
for key in user_hash_keys
      puts key
end
puts  "\n\nuser_hash_values  array  -  Length:  #{
user_hash_values.length() }\n\n"
for value in user_hash_values
      puts value
end
```

Output:

```
F:\RubyScripts>ruby hash_input.rb

Enter a key at index 0:
name

Enter the value at key name:
Iliza

Enter a key at index 1:
age

Enter the value at key age:
32

Enter a key at index 2:
occupation

Enter the value at key occupation:
IT Analyst

Enter a key at index 3:
city

Enter the value at key city:
Phoenix

Enter a key at index 4:
state

Enter the value at key state:
Arizona


Hash user_hash - Length: 5 - Complete Dump

 {"name"=>"Iliza", "age"=>"32", "occupation"=>"IT Analyst", "city"=>"Phoenix", "
state"=>"Arizona"}


user_hash_keys array - Length: 5

name
age
occupation
city
state


user_hash_values array - Length: 5

Iliza
32
IT Analyst
Phoenix
Arizona
```

Hashes are very useful data structures. How you use them is left up to you. You can store many details of one object or one detail of many objects.

14. Ranges

A range is a data set having a collection of items in a sequence. Items can be of any compatible data type such as numbers, alphabets, etc.

14.1 Range creation

A range can be created using ***range operators*** given by ***two dots (..)*** or ***three dots (…)***. ***Two dots (..)*** are used when the extreme value of the range is to be included and ***three dots (…)*** are to be used when the extreme value of the range is to be excluded. General syntax:

> *<variable> = (<range beginning> .. <range end>)*
> #OR
> *<variable> = (<range beginning> .. <range end>)*
> *Example:*
> *Numbers = (1..5)*
> *Alpha = ('a'…'h')*

When we say ***Numbers = (1..5)***, the variable will be filled with numbers ***1, 2, 3, 4 and 5***. The statement ***Alpha = ('a' … 'h')*** uses ***three dots (…)*** and will fill the variable ***Alpha*** with alphabets ***'a', 'b', 'c', 'd', 'e', 'f' and 'g'***. Note that ***'h' is excluded*** because we have used triple dots which excludes the extreme value.

Note: Ranges can only be created in ascending order and not in descending order.

Although a range is a collection of sequential items, it is not the same as an array although at a conceptually abstracted level it may seem so. However, a range can be converted to an array using the function ***to_a()***. General syntax:

<array variable> = <range variable>.to_a( )

Example:

Numbers_arr = Numbers.to_a( )

Let us write a Ruby script to demonstrate range creation and conversion to an array:

```
#Range Demo
#Create a numeric range
range1 = (1..10)
#Convert range to array
range1_arr = range1.to_a()
puts "range1 - #{ range1 } \nrange1_arr - #{ range1_arr } \nrange1_arr length - #{ range1_arr.length() }\n"
#Create an alphabetical range
alpha_range1 = ('i'..'q')
#Convert range to array
alpha_range1_arr = alpha_range1.to_a()
puts "\nalpha_range1 - #{ alpha_range1 } \nalpha_range1_arr - #{ alpha_range1_arr } \nalpha_range1_arr length - #{ alpha_range1_arr.length() }\n"
#Create an alphabetical range
alpha_range2 = ('A'..'E')
#Convert range to array
alpha_range2_arr = alpha_range2.to_a()
puts "\nalpha_range2 - #{ alpha_range2 } \nalpha_range2_arr - #{ alpha_range2_arr } \nalpha_range2_arr length - #{ alpha_range2_arr.length() }\n"
```

<u>Output:</u>

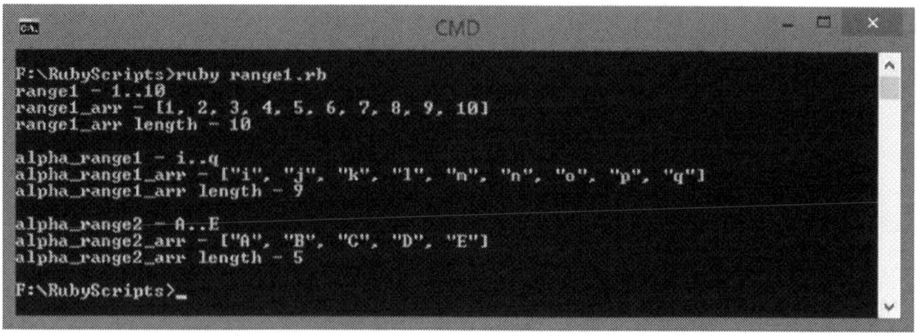

```
F:\RubyScripts>ruby range1.rb
range1 - 1..10
range1_arr - [1, 2, 3, 4, 5, 6, 7, 8, 9, 10]
range1_arr length - 10

alpha_range1 - i..q
alpha_range1_arr - ["i", "j", "k", "l", "m", "n", "o", "p", "q"]
alpha_range1_arr length - 9

alpha_range2 - A..E
alpha_range2_arr - ["A", "B", "C", "D", "E"]
alpha_range2_arr length - 5

F:\RubyScripts>_
```

A *for* loop can be used to iterate through a range variable without having to convert it to an array first. Here is an example:

```
#Ranges and loops
#Create a range in descending order
range1 = (-3..3)
#Create an alphabetical range, exclude the extreme value
alpha_range1 = ('a'...'d')
#Descending order alphabetical range
alpha_range2 = ('O'..'Z')
#Use loops to print range contents
puts "\nrange1 contents using for loop:\n"
for value in range1
      puts value
end
puts "\nalpha_range1 contents using for loop:\n"
for value in alpha_range1
      puts value
end
puts "\nalpha_range2 contents using for loop:\n"
for value in alpha_range2
      puts value
end
```

Output:

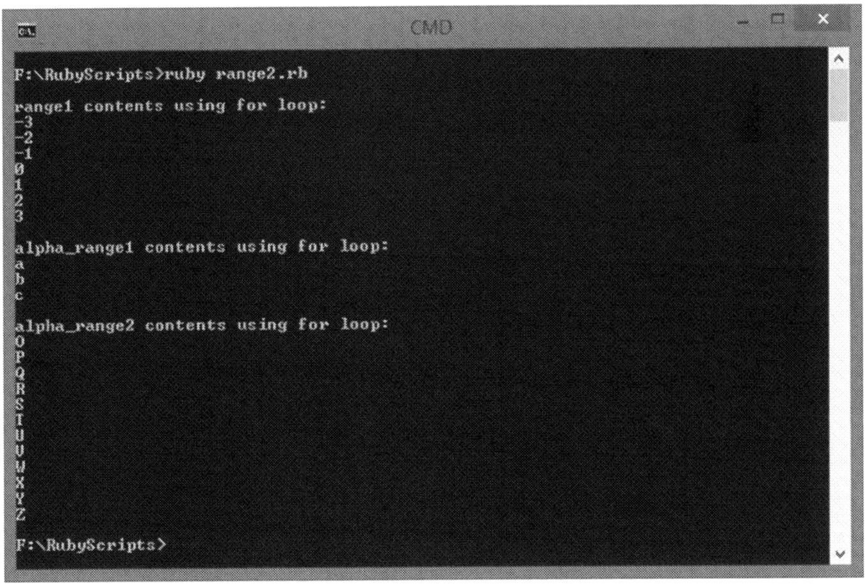

```
F:\RubyScripts>ruby range2.rb

range1 contents using for loop:
-3
-2
-1
0
1
2
3

alpha_range1 contents using for loop:
a
b
c

alpha_range2 contents using for loop:
O
P
Q
R
S
T
U
V
W
X
Y
Z

F:\RubyScripts>
```

14.2 Using Ranges in decision making

Ranges can be used in ***if-elsif-else*** constructs as well as in ***case-when*** constructs. Let us first take a look at ***case-when*** construct. General syntax:

case (<variable>)

when (<range 1 begin> … <range 1 end>)

#Statements to be executed when <variable> falls in range 1

when (<range 2 begin> … <range 2 end>)

#Statements to be executed when <variable> falls in range 2

when (<range 3 begin> … <range 3 end>)

#Statements to be executed when <variable> falls in range 3

when (<range 4 begin> … <range 4 end>)

#Statements to be executed when <variable> falls in range 4

…

…

…

when (<range n begin> … <range n end>)

#Statements to be executed when <variable> falls in range n

else

#Statements to be executed when <variable> does not fall in any range.

end

We have seen how a ***case-when*** construct works in the control structures chapter. The ***case*** statement is given an ***expression*** and ***when*** statements are given constant expressions. When the result of the expression matches one of the constant expressions of the ***when*** statements, that particular ***when block*** is executed. If no match is found, the ***else block*** is executed if it is present. When using ranges with ***case-when*** construct, the ***case*** statement is supplied with a variable or an expression. In the above code snippet, ***<variable>*** is used to keep things simple instead of an expression. The ***when*** statements are given ranges. If ***<variable>*** falls in between any of the ranges of the ***when*** statements, that particular ***when block*** will be executed. If no match is found, the ***else*** block will be executed.

Let us write a Ruby script to accept a number from the user and check which 10 number block does it fall between -50 and +50. The 10 number blocks will be -50 to -40, -40 to -30, … 0 to 10, … 40 to 50.

```
#Range and case when
#Prompt the user to enter a number
puts "\nEnter a number: "
num_str = gets
num_str = num_str.chomp
#Convert num_str to int formats
num = num_str.to_i()
case (num)
    when (-50..-40)
        puts "\n#{ num } falls between -50 and -40\n"
    when (-40..-30)
        puts "\n#{ num } falls between -40 and -30\n"
    when (-30..-20)
        puts "\n#{ num } falls between -30 and -20\n"
    when (-20..-10)
        puts "\n#{ num } falls between -20 and -10\n"
    when (-10..0)
        puts "\n#{ num } falls between -10 and 0\n"
    when (0..10)
        puts "\n#{ num } falls between 0 and 10\n"
    when (10..20)
        puts "\n#{ num } falls between 10 and 20\n"
    when (20..30)
        puts "\n#{ num } falls between 20 and 30\n"
    when (30..40)
        puts "\n#{ num } falls between 30 and 40\n"
    when (40..50)
        puts "\n#{ num } falls between 40 and 50\n"
    else
        puts "\n#{ num } does not fall anywhere
        between -50 and 50\n"
end
```

Output:

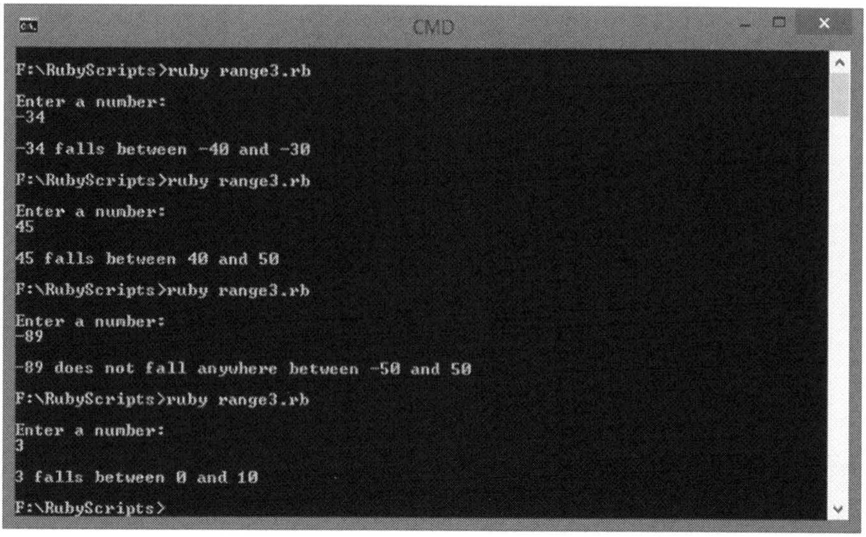

```
F:\RubyScripts>ruby range3.rb
Enter a number:
-34
-34 falls between -40 and -30
F:\RubyScripts>ruby range3.rb
Enter a number:
45
45 falls between 40 and 50
F:\RubyScripts>ruby range3.rb
Enter a number:
-89
-89 does not fall anywhere between -50 and 50
F:\RubyScripts>ruby range3.rb
Enter a number:
3
3 falls between 0 and 10
F:\RubyScripts>
```

The ***if-elsif-else*** construct can also be used to check if a variable falls between a particular range. To do so, we have to use the ***case equality*** operator given by ***three equal-to signs (===)***. This operator is informally known as *threequals*. General syntax:

if ((<range begin> .. <range end>) === <variable/value>)

#Statements to be executed if <variable/value> is in the given range.

end

Example:

if (('A' .. 'D') === alpha)

puts "#{ alpha } is between A and D"

end

Let us re-write the Ruby program used to demonstrate the working of ranges with ***case-when*** construct with ***if-elsif-else*** construct:

```
#Range and if else
#Prompt the user to enter a number
puts "\nEnter a number: "
num_str = gets
num_str = num_str.chomp
#Convert num_str to int formats
num = num_str.to_i()
if ((-50..-40) === num)
          puts "\n#{ num } falls between -50 and -40\n"
     elsif ((-40..-30) === num)
          puts "\n#{ num } falls between -40 and -30\n"
     elsif ((-30..-20) === num)
          puts "\n#{ num } falls between -30 and -20\n"
     elsif ((-20..-10) === num)
          puts "\n#{ num } falls between -20 and -10\n"
     elsif ((-10..0) === num)
          puts "\n#{ num } falls between -10 and 0\n"
     elsif ((0..10) === num)
          puts "\n#{ num } falls between 0 and 10\n"
     elsif ((10..20) === num)
          puts "\n#{ num } falls between 10 and 20\n"
     elsif ((20..30) === num)
          puts "\n#{ num } falls between 20 and 30\n"
     elsif ((30..40) === num)
          puts "\n#{ num } falls between 30 and 40\n"
     elsif ((40..50) === num)
          puts "\n#{ num } falls between 40 and 50\n"
     else
          puts "\n#{ num } does not fall anywhere
          between -50 and 50\n"
end
```

Output:

```
CMD

F:\RubyScripts>ruby range4.rb

Enter a number:
99

99 does not fall anywhere between -50 and 50

F:\RubyScripts>ruby range4.rb

Enter a number:
-5

-5 falls between -10 and 0

F:\RubyScripts>ruby range4.rb

Enter a number:
23

23 falls between 20 and 30

F:\RubyScripts>
```

As a fun exercise, let us write a Ruby script to accept an alphabet from the user and check whether it is in upper-case or lower-case:

```
#Range Upper and Lower case
#Prompt the user to enter an alphabet
puts "\nEnter an alphabet: "
alpha = gets
alpha =alpha.chomp
if (('a'..'z') === alpha)
      puts "\n#{ alpha } is in lower case.\n"
elsif (('A'..'Z') === alpha)
      puts "\n#{ alpha } is in upper case.\n"
else
      puts "\nInvalid input. Only single alphabets are
allowed.\n\n"
end
```

Output:

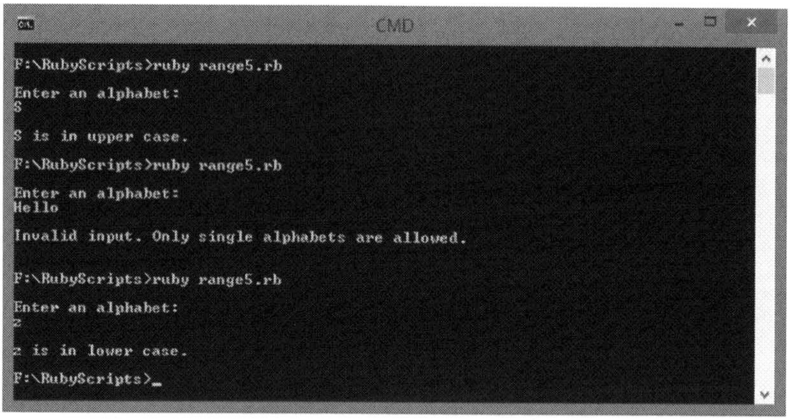

```
CMD

F:\RubyScripts>ruby range5.rb

Enter an alphabet:
S

S is in upper case.

F:\RubyScripts>ruby range5.rb

Enter an alphabet:
Hello

Invalid input. Only single alphabets are allowed.

F:\RubyScripts>ruby range5.rb

Enter an alphabet:
z

z is in lower case.

F:\RubyScripts>_
```

Note: When using ***triple equal-to sign (===)***, the operand on the left hand side should be the range. Both operands are not interchangeable.

15. Strings

A string is a sequence of characters. We have dealt with strings throughout this book. Let us revise a few concepts before moving ahead with string operations. A string can be declared by enclosing a sequence of characters within single quotes or double quotes. General syntax:

> *<string variable> = "<characters>"*
> #OR
> *<string variable> = '<characters>'*
> *Example:*
> *laptop_make = "MSI"*

Individual characters of a string can be accessed using the ***access operator ([<index>])*** just like in arrays. The escape character sequence begins with ***backslash (\)***. It is used to print restricted characters.

15.1 String Length

The length of a string can be determined using the ***size*** function as follows:

> *<length> = <string variable>.size*
> *Example:*
> *Len = laptop_make.size*

15.2 String Concatenation

More than one strings can be joined together using the ***concatenation operator (<<)***. General syntax:

> *<new string> = [string 1] << [string 2] << … << [string n]*
> *Example:*
> *name = first_name << " " << last_name*

Let us write a simple Ruby script to demonstrate the basics of strings:

```
#String Demo
#Declare a few strings
city = "Dubai"
country = "United Arab Emirates"
#Fetch size
city_length = city.size
country_length = country.size
#Print
puts "\ncity: #{ city } length: #{ city_length }"
puts "\ncountry: #{ country } length: #{ country_length }"
#Concatenate
address = city << " , " << country
address_length = address.size
puts "\naddress: #{ address } length: #{ address_length }\n"
#Use while loop to print city
index = 0
while (index < city_length)
      puts "\nindex: #{ index } character: #{ city[index] }"
      index = index + 1
end
```

<u>Output:</u>

```
CMD
F:\RubyScripts>ruby stringdemo.rb
city: Dubai length: 5
country: United Arab Emirates length: 20
address: Dubai , United Arab Emirates length: 28
index: 0 character: D
index: 1 character: u
index: 2 character: b
index: 3 character: a
index: 4 character: i
F:\RubyScripts>
```

15.3 Substring

A substring can be extracted from a string by using the access operator in the following way:

<substring var> = <string>[<start index>, <number of characters>]

Example:

msg = "Hello World"

x = msg[6, 5]

In the above example, ***W*** is at index ***6*** and ***5*** characters from there will get you ***W,o,r,l*** and ***d***. Hence, ***msg[6, 5]*** will fetch the substring ***"World"***.

15.4 Convert to Upper and Lower case

The functions ***upcase*** and ***downcase*** are used to convert all characters of a string to upper case and lower case respectively. General syntax:

<variable> = <string>.upcase

<variable> = <string>.downcase

Example:

data = msg.upcase

data = msg.downcase

Here is a Ruby script that demonstrates how to extract a substring from another string and how to convert a string to upper case and lower case:

```
#String Operations
#Declare a string
name = "Anna Watson"
#Extract substring
```

```
first_name = name[0, 4]
last_name = name[5, 6]
#Upper and lower case
name_uppercase = name.upcase
name_lowercase = name.downcase
#Print everything
puts "\nname: #{ name }"
puts "\nfirst_name: #{ first_name }"
puts "\nlast_name: #{ last_name }"
puts "\nname_uppercase: #{ name_uppercase }"
puts "\nname_lowercase: #{ name_lowercase } \n\n"
```

Output:

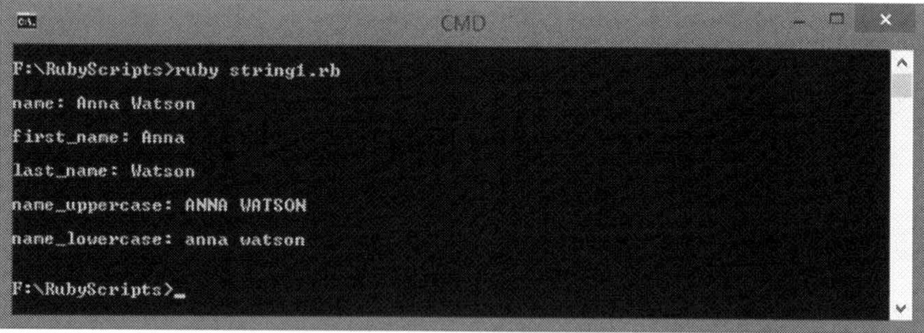

15.5 String Equality

Two strings can be compared and checked for equality using the equal-to comparison operator given by ***two equal-to signs (==).*** This operator will either result in ***true*** or ***false***. Note that Ruby is a case sensitive language. The words ***"Ruby"*** and ***"ruby"*** are not the same. If you compare ***"Ruby"*** == ***"ruby"***, the result will be ***false***. If there is such a situation where the case is not important, then it is a good idea to convert both strings to either lower case or upper case before comparing. Let us write a Ruby script to accept two strings from the user and check if they are the same:

```
#String equality
#Prompt the user to enter a string
puts "\nEnter a string: "
str1 = gets.chomp
```

```
puts "\nEnter another string: "
str2 = gets.chomp
if (str1 == str2)
	puts "\nBoth strings are the same.\n"
else
	puts "\nBoth strings are NOT the same. \n"
end
```

Output:

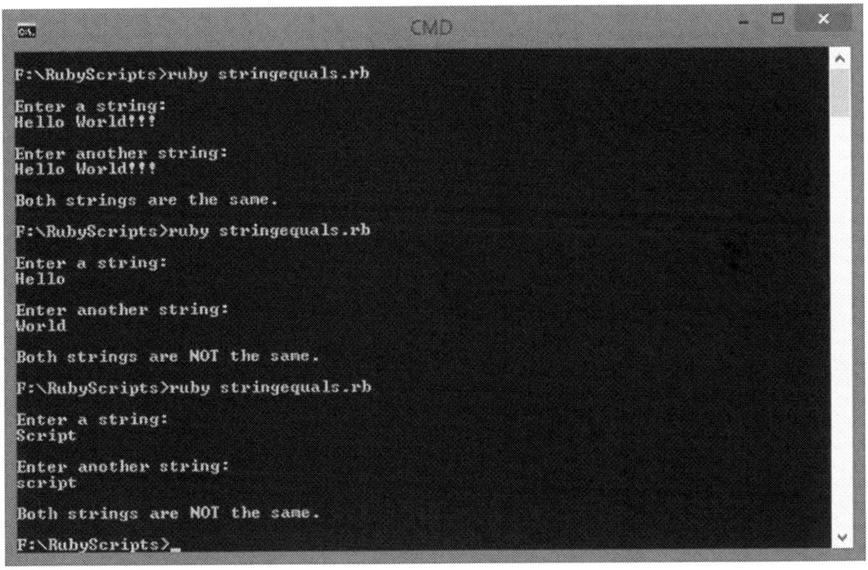

```
CMD

F:\RubyScripts>ruby stringequals.rb

Enter a string:
Hello World!!!

Enter another string:
Hello World!!!

Both strings are the same.

F:\RubyScripts>ruby stringequals.rb

Enter a string:
Hello

Enter another string:
World

Both strings are NOT the same.

F:\RubyScripts>ruby stringequals.rb

Enter a string:
Script

Enter another string:
script

Both strings are NOT the same.

F:\RubyScripts>_
```

15.6 String Search

A string can be searched for inside another string using the ***index*** function. General syntax:

> *<variable> = <string>.index(<string to be searched>)*
>
> *Example:*
>
> *location = msg.index("Ruby")*

The ***index*** function returns the location of the specified string. If the specified string is not found in the main string, this function returns ***nil***. Here is a Ruby script that accepts one string from the user and asks for the string to be searched. Performs string search operation using the ***index*** function and returns the result:

```
#String search
#Prompt the user to enter a string
puts "\nEnter a string: "
str1 = gets.chomp
puts "\nEnter the string to be searched: "
str2 = gets.chomp
loc = str1.index(str2)
if (loc != nil)
      puts "\n#{ str2 } has been found at index: #{ loc
}\n"
else
      puts "\n#{ str2 } has not been found \n"
end
```

<u>Output:</u>

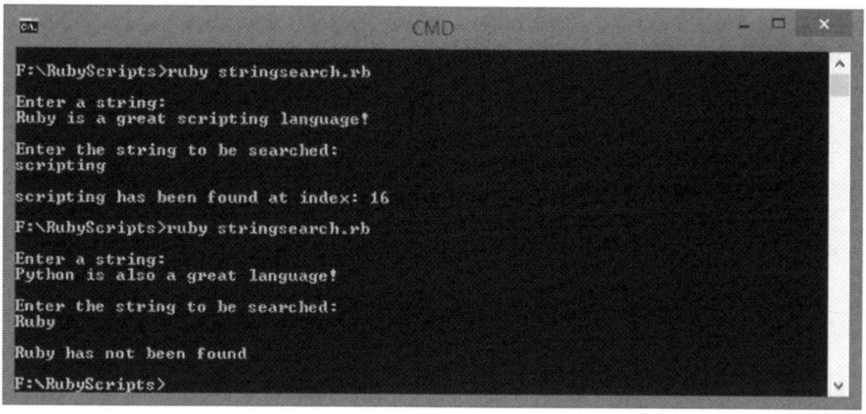

```
CMD
F:\RubyScripts>ruby stringsearch.rb

Enter a string:
Ruby is a great scripting language!

Enter the string to be searched:
scripting

scripting has been found at index: 16

F:\RubyScripts>ruby stringsearch.rb

Enter a string:
Python is also a great language!

Enter the string to be searched:
Ruby

Ruby has not been found

F:\RubyScripts>
```

16. Introduction to Classes and Objects

In ***Chapter*** *6*, we learned the basics of Object Oriented Programming paradigm. That was only a basic chapter just to introduce a new programming paradigm. In this chapter, we will learn how to define our own classes and objects. Covering all of OOP using Ruby is not possible and hence only the introductory concepts about classes and objects are covered. This chapter is very important if you want to learn some of the advanced Ruby stuff like ***Ruby on Rails*** for web development.

16.1 Class Definition

A class is a definition of user defined data type. It may or may not contain data. Inside a class, you can have ***variables*** (***data members)*** called ***instance variables*** and ***member functions or methods*** to work on those data members. An ***object*** is an instance of a class which has its own copy of ***instance variables***. Instance variables begin with ***at the rate (@)*** sign. There is another type of variables called ***class variables***. These are equivalent to static variables in the OOP domain. Class variables are shared by all objects. These begin with ***double at the rate signs (@@).***

A class can be defined using the ***class*** keyword as shown below:

```
class <ClassName>
        #Statements
end
Example:
class DemoClass
        #Do nothing here
end
```

Note: The class name should always start with an upper case letter.

There are a few categories of class methods. We will take a look at the important ones.

16.2 Constructor – initialize method

The ***initialize method*** is the ***constructor*** of the class. This method gets invoked every time an object is created. This method is defined inside the class just like any other method with the help of a ***def*** keyword. The name of this method should be ***initialize***, no other names are permitted and it may or may not accept parameters. General syntax:

```
class <ClassName>
        def initialize()
                #Statements to be executed when an object is created.
        end
end
Example:
class DemoClass
        def initialize()
                puts "Object created!"
        end
end
```

The initialize method can be used to initialize instance variables in the following way. For this, you will have to write this method to accept parameters. Although you could do without parameters and assign some hard coded values to instance variables but accepting parameters and assigning makes a lot more sense. Here is how you would do it:

```
class <ClassName>
        def initialize(<param 1>, <param 2>, … <param n>)
                @<instance var 2> = <param 1>
                @<instance var 2> = <param 2>
                …
                @<instance var n> = <param n>
                #Statements to be executed when an object is created.
        end
end
Example:
class DemoClass
        def initialize(x, y, z)
                @a = x
                @b = y
                @c = z
        end
end
```

In the above example, the initialize method accepts three arguments – ***x, y and z***. When an object is created and these parameters are passed, the initialize method will be invoked and inside it, ***x, y and z*** will be assigned to instance variable ***@a, @b and @c*** respectively.

16.3 Object Creation

An object can be created using the ***new*** keyword. General syntax:

```
<object variable> = <Class name>.new
Example:
obj = DemoClass.new
```

When the ***initialize*** method of a class does not accept any arguments, a simple ***new*** keyword will suffice as shown in the example above. Whereas, when the ***initialize*** method is defined to accept parameters, *the exact number of parameters should be passed (and in that order)* using the ***new*** keyword as shown below:

<object variable> = <Class name>.new(<param 1>, <param 2>, … <param n>)

Example:

obj = MyClass.new (1, 2, 3)

Let us write a simple class with an ***initialize*** method that does not accept any arguments just to check what happens when an object is created.

```
#Class Demo
#Define a class
class MyClass
      def initialize()
            puts "\nObject created!"
      end
end
#Script execution begins here
#Create 3 objects of MyClass type
x = MyClass.new
y = MyClass.new
z = MyClass.new
```

Output:

```
CMD
F:\RubyScripts>ruby classdemo.rb
Object created!
Object created!
Object created!
F:\RubyScripts>_
```

As see, we are creating three objects of ***MyClass*** type and hence the ***initialize*** method gets invoked three times.

16.4 Accessor methods

Accessor methods are used to retrieve the values of ***instance variables***. These are also known as ***getter methods*** or ***getters***. Note that instance variables cannot be accessed directly and need such methods to do so. One accessor method can retrieve only one variable at a time though there is no restriction on the data type of a variable. Hence, if you want to access multiple values, you can easily put them inside an array, hash, etc. Here is the syntax to write an accessor method:

```
class <ClassName>
        def <accessor method>()
                @<variable to be accessed>
        end
end
Example:
class DemoClass
        def getName()
                @Name
        end
end
```

When an object of a class is created (using the new keyword and thereby invoking the initialize method as shown in the previous section), the accessor methods can be invoked in the following ways:

```
<variable> = <object name>.<accessor method>( )
```

Example:
Obj = DemoClass.new
Name = Obj.getName( )

The getter methods return the specified variable back to the calling statement and hence there should be a variable to receive that value. Without that, the returned value will be lost. You can alternatively directly print the returned value if it is in printable format with the help of string substitution using ***puts*** function as follows:

puts "#{ <object name>.<accessor method>( ) }
Example:
puts "#{ Obj.getName( ) }

Note: The instance variables should be initialized first either using the ***initialize method*** or using ***setter methods*** (covered in the next section).

Let us write a Ruby script to define a class, initialize a few instance variables using the initialize method and write a few getter methods to retrieve each of those variables.

```
#Classes and Objects Demo
#Using accessor methods
class Person
	#Constructor - initialize method
	def initialize(f_name, l_name, age, country)
		@first_name = f_name
		@last_name = l_name
		@age = age
		@country = country
	end
	#Accessor method to retrieve first_name
	def getFirstName()
		@first_name
	end
	#Accessor method to retrieve last_name
```

```
        def getLastName()
                @last_name
        end
        #Accessor method to retrieve age
        def getAge()
                @age
        end
        #Accessor method to retrieve country
        def getCountry()
                @country
        end
end
#Script execution begins here
#Create 2 objects of class Person
p1 = Person.new("Monica", "Ford", 23, "USA")
p2 = Person.new("Albert", "Lemon", 41, "UK")
#Print details of p1 and p2 using accessor methods of
class Person
puts "\n\nObject - p1\nfirst_name: #{ p1.getFirstName
}\nlast_name: #{ p1.getLastName }\nage: #{ p1.getAge
}\ncountry: #{ p1.getCountry }\n"
puts "\n\nObject - p2\nfirst_name: #{ p2.getFirstName
}\nlast_name: #{ p2.getLastName }\nage: #{ p2.getAge
}\ncountry: #{ p2.getCountry }\n"
```

Output:

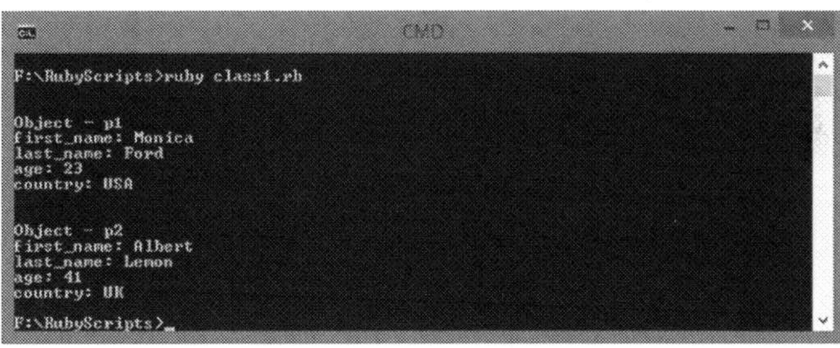

16.4 Setter methods

Setter methods are used to set values of instance variables. Setter methods can be defined inside a class using the ***def*** keyword as follows:

class <ClassName>

def <setter method name>=(<parameter>)

@<variable to be set> = <parameter>

end

end

Example:

class DemoClass

def setName=(name)

@Name = name

end

end

When an object of a class is created the setter methods can be invoked to set the values of instance variables in the following way:

< <object name>.<setter method> = <value>

Example:

Obj = DemoClass.new

Obj.setName = "Carl"

Let us modify the previous example. After initializing the objects, let us change the values of instance variables using setter methods:

```
#Classes and Objects Demo
#Using setter methods
class Person
      #Constructor - initialize method
      def initialize(f_name, l_name, age, country)
            @first_name = f_name
            @last_name = l_name
            @age = age
            @country = country
      end
      #Accessor method to retrieve first_name
      def getFirstName()
            @first_name
      end
```

```
    #Accessor method to retrieve last_name
    def getLastName()
        @last_name
    end
    #Accessor method to retrieve age
    def getAge()
        @age
    end
    #Accessor method to retrieve country
    def getCountry()
        @country
    end
    #Setter method to set first_name
    def setFirstName=(f_name)
        @first_name = f_name
    end
    #Setter method to set last_name
    def setLastName=(l_name)
        @last_name = l_name
    end
    #Setter method to set age
    def setAge=(age)
        @age = age
    end
    #Setter method to set country
    def setCountry=(country)
        @country = country
    end
end
#Script execution begins here
#Create 2 objects of class Person
p1 = Person.new("Janice", "Lambert", 31, "Denmark")
p2 = Person.new("Bianca", "Mathews", 19, "Brazil")
#Print details of p1 and p2 using accessor methods of
class Person
puts "\n\nObject - p1\nfirst_name: #{ p1.getFirstName
}\nlast_name: #{ p1.getLastName }\nage: #{ p1.getAge
}\ncountry: #{ p1.getCountry }\n"
puts "\n\nObject - p2\nfirst_name: #{ p2.getFirstName
}\nlast_name: #{ p2.getLastName }\nage: #{ p2.getAge
}\ncountry: #{ p2.getCountry }\n"
#Edit details
p1.setFirstName = "Candice"
p2.setLastName = "Reyez"
p1.setAge = 33
p2.setCountry = "Peru"
puts "\n\nAfter editing using setter methods\n"
```

```
#Print details of p1 and p2 using accessor methods of
class Person after editing
puts "\n\nObject - p1\nfirst_name: #{ p1.getFirstName
}\nlast_name: #{ p1.getLastName }\nage: #{ p1.getAge
}\ncountry: #{ p1.getCountry }\n"
puts "\n\nObject - p2\nfirst_name: #{ p2.getFirstName
}\nlast_name: #{ p2.getLastName }\nage: #{ p2.getAge
}\ncountry: #{ p2.getCountry }\n"
```

Output:

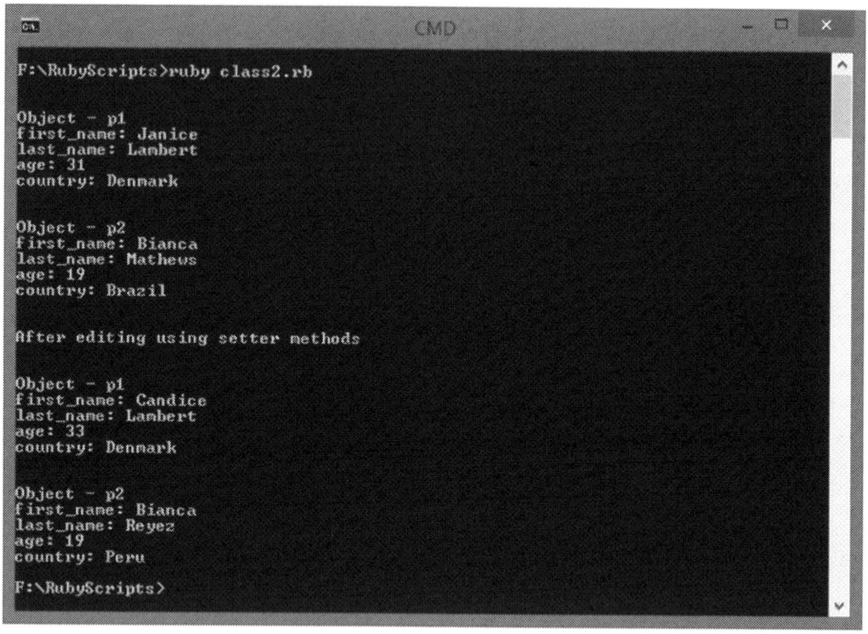

```
CMD
F:\RubyScripts>ruby class2.rb


Object - p1
first_name: Janice
last_name: Lambert
age: 31
country: Denmark


Object - p2
first_name: Bianca
last_name: Mathews
age: 19
country: Brazil


After editing using setter methods


Object - p1
first_name: Candice
last_name: Lambert
age: 33
country: Denmark


Object - p2
first_name: Bianca
last_name: Reyez
age: 19
country: Peru

F:\RubyScripts>
```

The above two examples were using hard coded values. Let us write a Ruby script to accept details of a person and then dynamically create an object with those values:

```
#Classes and Objects Demo
class Person
	#Constructor - initialize method
	def initialize(f_name, l_name, age, country)
		@first_name = f_name
		@last_name = l_name
		@age = age
		@country = country
```

```
    end
    #Accessor method to retrieve first_name
    def getFirstName()
        @first_name
    end
    #Accessor method to retrieve last_name
    def getLastName()
        @last_name
    end
    #Accessor method to retrieve age
    def getAge()
        @age
    end
    #Accessor method to retrieve country
    def getCountry()
        @country
    end
end
#Script execution begins here
puts "Enter first name: "
first_name = gets
puts "Enter last name: "
last_name = gets
puts "Enter age: "
age = gets
puts "Enter your country: "
country = gets
#Chomp all inputs
first_name = first_name.chomp
last_name = last_name.chomp
age = age.chomp.to_i()
country = country.chomp
#Create an object of class Person
p = Person.new(first_name, last_name, age, country)
#Print details of p using accessor methods of class
Person
puts "\n\nObject - p\nfirst_name: #{ p.getFirstName
}\nlast_name: #{ p.getLastName }\nage: #{ p.getAge
}\ncountry: #{ p.getCountry }\n"
```

Output:

```
F:\RubyScripts>ruby class_user_input.rb
Enter first name:
Rohan
Enter last name:
Singh
Enter  age:
26
Enter your country:
India


Object - p
first_name: Rohan
last_name: Singh
age: 26
country: India

F:\RubyScripts>
```

Here are a few important points to remember in this chapter:

- A class block begins with the ***class*** keyword and ends with an ***end*** keyword.
- A class name should start with an upper case letter. Numbers and underscores are permitted but it is best to use alphabets only, perhaps use camel case. Eg. ***MyClass, PersonClass, LaptopClass,*** etc.
- Initializer method is used to initialize objects. These methods get invoked when an object is created. It is not mandatory to have an initializer method, your program will work just fine without one but it is a very useful feature and a good programming practice to use constructors to initialize objects.
- Accessor methods are used to fetch values of instance variables, only one variable can be accessed at a time. Setter methods are used to set values to variables, only one variable can be set at a time.

17. Programming Examples

Now that we have learned the basics of Ruby, let us take a look at a few programming examples.

17.1 Fibonacci Series

A Fibonacci series begins with the terms 0 and 1. The next term is derived by adding the previous two terms. The series looks like this 0, 1, 1, 2, 3, 5, 8, 13, 21, … Let us write a script to generate this series.

```
#Fibonacci series
puts "Enter the number of terms to be generated: "
num_str = gets
num = num_str.chomp.to_i()
prev = 0;
current = 1;
puts "\nFibonacci Series: \n\n";
#Generate Fibo series
puts " #{ prev } \n #{ current }";
i = 0
while (i < num - 2)
      nxt = prev + current ;
      puts " #{ nxt } "
      prev = current;
      current = nxt;
      i += 1
end
puts "\n"
```

Output:

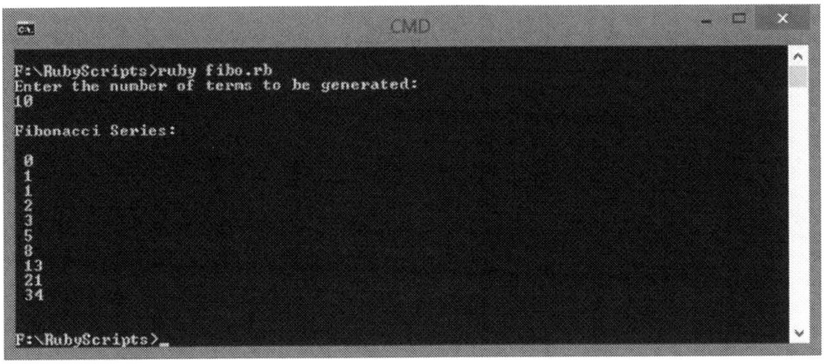

```
CMD
F:\RubyScripts>ruby fibo.rb
Enter the number of terms to be generated:
10

Fibonacci Series:

 0
 1
 1
 2
 3
 5
 8
 13
 21
 34

F:\RubyScripts>_
```

17.2 Factorial

The factorial of a number n is represented as $n!$ where $n! = n \times (n - 1) \times (n - 2) \times \ldots 1$. For example – factorial of 4 is represented as $4! = 4 \times 3 \times 2 \times 1 = 24$. Factorial of 0 is 1 and it is not possible to calculate factorial of a negative number. Let us write a Ruby script to accept a number form the user and compute its factorial.

```
#Factorial
puts "\nEnter a number: "
num_str = gets
num = num_str.chomp.to_i()
if (num >=0 )
      fact = 1
      i = num
      while (i > 1)
            fact = fact * i
            i -= 1
      end
      puts "\nFactorial of #{ num } is #{ fact }\n"
else
      puts "\nFactorial of a negative number cannot be
calculated.\n"
end
```

Output:

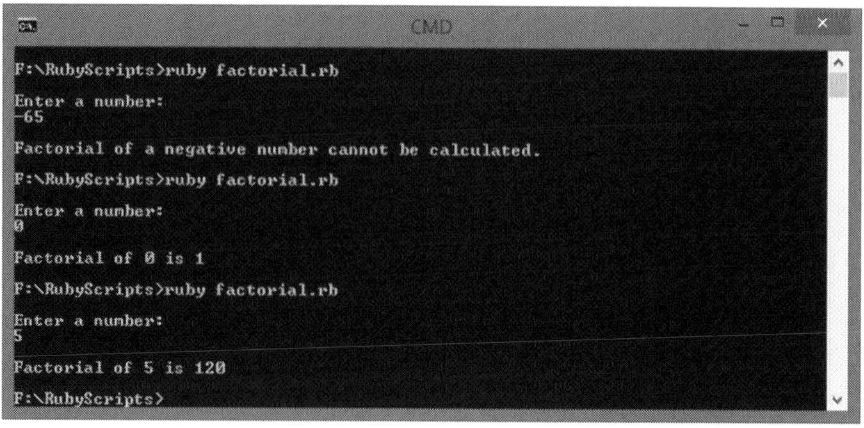

```
CMD
F:\RubyScripts>ruby factorial.rb

Enter a number:
-65

Factorial of a negative number cannot be calculated.

F:\RubyScripts>ruby factorial.rb

Enter a number:
0

Factorial of 0 is 1

F:\RubyScripts>ruby factorial.rb

Enter a number:
5

Factorial of 5 is 120

F:\RubyScripts>
```

17.3 Reverse an array

Let us write a program to accept 5 values from the user, put them in an array and reverse it.

```
#Array Reversal
#Declare an empty array of 5 elements
arr = Array.new(5)
#Initialize a loop variable
index = 0
#Loop for 5 times, read 5 values as inputs
while (index < arr.length) do
      #Read array elements
      #Prompt the user to enter an element
      puts "\nEnter an element at index #{ index }: \n"
      str = gets
      str = str.chomp
      #Add str to arr at current index
      arr[index] = str
      #Increment loop variable
      index = index + 1
end
#Create another array to store the reverse
#Declare an empty array of 5 elements
rev_arr = Array.new(5)
i = 4
j = 0
while (j < arr.length) do
      rev_arr[i] = arr[j]
      j += 1
      i -= 1
end
puts "\nOriginal array: \n#{ arr } \n\nReversed array:
\n#{ rev_arr }\n"
```

Output:

```
F:\RubyScripts>ruby arrayrev.rb

Enter an element at index 0:
Hello

Enter an element at index 1:
5

Enter an element at index 2:
Russia

Enter an element at index 3:
-8.4

Enter an element at index 4:
Berlin

Original array:
["Hello", "5", "Russia", "-8.4", "Berlin"]

Reversed array:
["Berlin", "-8.4", "Russia", "5", "Hello"]

F:\RubyScripts>_
```

17.4 Sum of all digits of a number

Let us read a number from the user and calculate the sum of all digits. The trick is to extract the last digit using ***num % 10*** and then discard it using ***num / 10***. Since integer on integer division is performed, the statement ***num / 10*** will discard the last digit. This process should go on in an iterative manner.

```
#Sum of all digits
puts "\nEnter a number: "
num_str = gets
num = num_str.chomp.to_i()
#Initialize a variable to store sum
sum = 0
#Loop while num is greater than 0
while (num > 0) do
      sum = sum + (num % 10)
      num = num / 10
end
puts "\nThe sum of all digits is: #{ sum } \n"
```

Output:

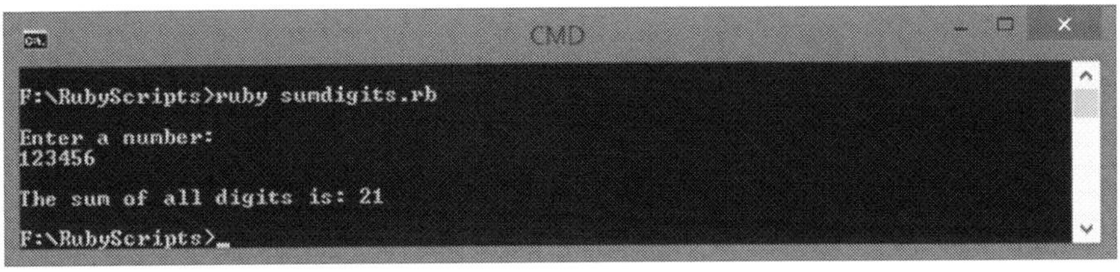

```
CMD
F:\RubyScripts>ruby sumdigits.rb

Enter a number:
123456

The sum of all digits is: 21

F:\RubyScripts>_
```

17.5 Reverse a number

Let us write a Ruby script to read a number from the user and reverse it. We will use the same trick mentioned in the previous program.

```
#Reverse a given number
puts "\nEnter a number: "
num_str = gets
num = num_str.chomp.to_i()
#Initialize a variable to store reverse
rev = 0
#Loop while num is greater than 0
while (num > 0) do
      #Multiply 10 to rev to take the reverse to the
next place
      #Add one's digit to rev
      rev = (rev * 10 ) + ( num % 10 ) ;
      #Discard one's digit. Use int integer by integer
division
      num = num / 10 ;

end
puts "\nReverse: #{ rev } \n"
```

Output:

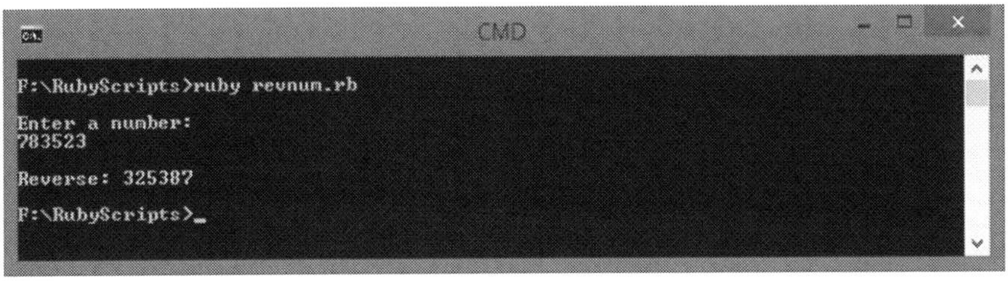

```
CMD
F:\RubyScripts>ruby revnum.rb

Enter a number:
783523

Reverse: 325387

F:\RubyScripts>_
```

18. Final Thoughts

In this book, I have tried my best to cover the basic concepts of Ruby. The programming examples covered in each topic are very basic and just enough to give you a good understanding of the topic in question. Once you have understood those programs, I suggest you make changes to the programs and see how the scripts behave in different scenarios.

Ruby is a powerful language, you can do a lot of things with it although it is mostly used for web application development and REST API development. If you want to learn more about Ruby, I suggest you take a look at some of the more advanced topics such as file handling, exception handling, advanced object oriented programming, etc. Those of you who are web developers, I strongly suggest learning OOP using Ruby well and then proceeding to learn a framework called ***Ruby on Rails (RoR).*** If you want to pursue web development using Ruby without prior web knowledge, I suggest you learn basic web technologies such as HTML, CSS, JS, etc., learn to build basic web pages, deploy them on a server and then proceed with Ruby web development.

Hope you enjoyed reading this book as much as I enjoyed writing it!

Good Luck!

If you enjoyed this book as much as I've enjoyed writing it, you can subscribe* to my email list for exclusive content and sneak peaks of my future books.

Visit the link below:

http://eepurl.com/du_L4n

OR

Use the QR Code:

(*Must be 13 years or older to subscribe)

Printed in Great Britain
by Amazon

86014259R00087